Elite Seduction

Actionable Tools for *Love*, *Seduction*, and *Dating*

JOHNNY CASSELL

(with Nate Chai)

Visit the author's website at **www.JohnnyCassell.com**

Published by StoryWand, London

Helping busy entrepreneurs quickly produce and share their high-impact message. StoryWand. You Wave it, we Make it.

www.StoryWand.co

ISBN-13: 978-1-9160277-0-1

Elite Seduction

ACTIONABLE TOOLS FOR DATING, SEDUCTION, AND LOVE

Johnny Cassell

(with Nate Chai)

Contents

- The Truth About Why You're Holding Yourself Back from Meeting Your Dream Partner
- How Your Own Brain Tricks You into Dating Failure
- How to Train Yourself to Become an Automatic Seduction Machine

- Why Your "Friends" Are Tanking Your Dating Game
- The Secret to Becoming an Elite Seducer Quickly
- How to Effectively Analyse What's Getting in Your Way

To Work with Johnny and For more Advice Head over to

www.JohnnyCassell.com

Foreword

As the founder of *Killing Kittens* I've been at the forefront of helping women express their sexuality for 12 years with the goal of providing a safe space for women to control their sexuality and be *in* control of it. It was launched in a time when sex was still a taboo topic, but *Sex and the City* had just come out and opened up the conversation about sex toys, blow jobs, and the sexual dynamics of a male-female relationship.

That was a decade ago.

Within those 10 years, women's sexuality has been thrust out into the open alongside all the dating apps and high-street sex shops, and it's been fascinating watching the changes in how relationships, women, and the world of dating operates. With the speed of change in the dating and relationship sphere, we've had to constantly evolve how we communicate with our customers to ensure that we provide them with the same promise of safety and openness we made 10 years ago.

Now we have an overload of information in the digital world and in our lives. A lot of things are miscommunicated or misunderstood, and assumptions are made. Often these can be avoided by having a simple face-to-face communication or by using clear language. If a man can communicate clearly with a woman, then he's going to have a much easier time finding and building incredible life-changing relationships with the fairer sex.

However, most men don't communicate well with women, or they sit on the fence of relationships and lead women on, and then they wonder why all the women in their lives are so angry!

In the world we live in today, it's very difficult for men to communicate effectively because they have to tip toe around the feminist movement and what that stands for. Some women love having the door held open for them and the classic chivalrous behaviour, whilst others find that offensive.

It's a minefield for the modern man to understand what, when, and how they need to communicate with certain types of girls compared to another.

In this modern minefield, Johnny is your personal bomb disposal squad. Holding your hand through and clearing out all the potential problems, miscommunications, and bullshit that we face when speaking to the opposite sex.

What Johnny does is cut through all that bollocks, smoke and miscommunication. He gets old-school and teaches how to simply communicate no matter who the woman is or what she stands for, and in a way that leaves both parties having had a great interaction.

Emma Sayle
Founder of **Killing Kittens**

Introduction

Hi, my name's Johnny Cassell, and I want to thank you for picking up this book and deciding to make your life what you want it to be. You are about to go on a life-changing journey that will leave you with the ability to pick and choose which women you want in your life.

I've been a dating coach since 2007, and in that time I've travelled all over the world teaching people how to communicate with the opposite sex. I've had incredible sexual encounters that would make porn stars blush. And I've met, dated, and fallen in love with high-calibre women who usually turn down 99 percent of the men they meet.

But my life wasn't always like that.

I used to be *terrified* of women. As a child, I was viciously bullied by a set of girls, sending me home with bruises every other week. And as a teenager, I was a shy, gangly engineering student with terrible posture and lacking social confidence. I couldn't muster the courage to even *talk* to a woman.

I had one thing going for me – a belief that I *could* change. I knew *I* had to make the choice to make my life better. All I had to do was *admit* I needed help and be willing to *ask* for it.

Since I made that decision and, after more than 100,000 coaching hours, after more than leading 200 international seduction workshops, after helping more than 2,000 clients meet the woman of their dreams, and after *every single* one of my wing-men was married or in a long-term relationship, I felt it was time to write my techniques down.

I wrote this book to reach people like *you* – men seeking a better, brighter, more successful experience with women. The tools and insights in this book have been designed to provide you with a better lifestyle full of the social interactions that you want.

I honestly believe the more people who understand the principles and techniques you are about to discover in this book, the healthier relationship environment we all will be able to live in. I by no means claim to know everything, but I can guarantee what I do know will dramatically change your life. What you choose to do with the knowledge is completely up to you.

All I ask is that you respect others, be ethical and give those you choose to include in your journey an exciting experience.

Who This Book Is For

In my work, I specialize in working with particular kinds of clients. This book has been written with those men in mind. Here are the kind of men this book is for:

The guy who has sacrificed his social life to move ahead in his career. He is content financially, but now he wants to accelerate his social learning curve.

The guy who is caught up in the weekend millionaire lifestyle, or stuck in the "lad culture", where the main concern amongst his peers is where the next "piss up" is going to be.

The high achiever who is an absolute dragon in the board room but cannot muster an ounce worth of courage to talk to someone on the other side of the room.

The guy who has just come out of a long-term relationship and needs to brush up on his know-how and blow out the cobwebs.

The guy who appears to have it all figured out, yet on the inside there is a completely different story.

If you don't fit into any of the above archetypes, I'd suggest sending me an email (**info@johnnycassell.com**), so I can point you in the right direction.

However, if one or more of them apply to you, then read on. This book will change your life.

How to Read This Book

We all learn in different ways, so in order to help as many of you readers as possible, I've divided each chapter of this book into three sections: **stories**, **explanations**, and **techniques**. Each one of these sections will stimulate different parts of your brain.

The **stories** highlight my mindset at particular points in my life, giving you insight into *how* I was thinking and what I did to change it.

The **explanation** section delves into *why* the chapter topic is important and *what* to do with the knowledge.

The **techniques** section gives you actionable exercises and techniques to implement the chapter's larger principles in your own life.

Naturally, reading every section of each chapter will give you a better understanding of the topic as a whole. However, I understand we're all busy people, so dip in and out of the sections as you see fit.

Before We Begin

Here is your first exercise:

1. Take a sheet of A4 paper.
2. Divide it down the middle.
3. At the top of each section write "Visual" and "Character".
4. Now, list *every* trait you want in your ideal woman.

By "every trait" I mean *everything*! Be specific.

For "Visual", how much taller or shorter is she than you? What is her ethnic background? How long is her hair? Don't hold back. Build your dream woman.

For "Character", ask yourself things like, is she adventurous? Is she creative? What are the values that she holds dearest to herself? *Everything.*

Don't edit yourself. Be honest.

This exercise is designed to free you from any mental barriers you may be putting up. If you write down a trait and then think, "I couldn't get a girl like that," *that's* one of the mental barriers I'm talking about!

I want you to see in your mind's eye exactly who you want, and I want you to make this person your end goal. Everything

you do now is leading up to you meeting that person, and when you inevitably *do* meet, I want you to be ready.

Here's a brief example of what this should look like:

Visual:	Character:
Between 160cm and 170cm	Confident
Curvy	Adventurous
Deep green eyes	Curious
Redhead	Polite
	Kind
	Socially Conscious
	Good communicator
	Affectionate
	Honest
	Speaks her mind
	Intelligent

This is just a brief example of what a list should look like. As you gain more experiences with women, your list will grow and evolve as you realise things that you enjoy about people and things that you don't find attractive.

This list is to heighten our awareness. If I were to ask my friends what their type is they'd say "hot" or "blonde" or "brunette". Therefore they'd settle for average. If you describe what you want in an average manner, then you will only settle for average. If you describe in detail then you will achieve the expectional.

What This Book Is Going to Teach You

"Your only limit is your imagination."

The first time I heard that, I thought, *What a load of bullshit.* To me it sounded like some new-age nonsense people say to sell personal development courses.

However, when I finally began to understand what stimulates people's minds, I started to see the bigger picture, and I wanted to discover what was possible. So I began to experiment. That meant breaking expected patterns of social interactions by going out and creating conversations with the most bizarre ice breakers. A personal favourite was, *"If you could be a superhero and possess any given superpower, who would you be and what would your superpower be?"*

For me, what holds the most value in life is having the ability to find companionship. After all, I believe that's what we're all here for. All of the fun we have up until that point is all part of the journey.

From this book you're going to learn how to:

- Become your own personal dating coach;
- Know what to say when you first approach a woman;
- Understand the emotional mechanisms that lead to you getting the number, the kiss, and even same-day sex;
- Get high-quality women chasing *you* from the moment you walk into a bar; and
- Become the man you've always wanted to be.

When you allow yourself to experience what *is* possible, everything changes. You can go on to date the hottest girls in

the club, the hottest models, actresses and pop stars, and the best, highest-quality women in your city.

You can fulfil all your wildest fantasies and deepest sexual desires. You can create a highly influential circle of friends and a global power network. Again, what you choose to do with these tools is completely up to you.

Your only limit is your imagination.

CHAPTER ONE:
Taking Responsibility

---

*"You are in categories outside the ones you want to be in because **you put yourself there**. Quit blaming and making excuses. **Take ownership** of things you want."*
- Johnny Cassell

It's so easy to hide behind a pile of excuses as to why you can't excel in a certain area of your life. It's so easy to just accept that certain people won't like you. These are negative crutches.

I relied on similar crutches until I started taking responsibility for my actions. I realized if I wasn't taking control of my life, I would just be following someone else's reality.

You're probably in a situation in your life right now where you're going out every week, maybe a couple of nights a week, and you're not really in control of what you do and where you're going. But you're just being a sheep when you need to be the shepherd.

Being the shepherd means being a leader. It means taking control and knowing where you're going, and that is attractive.

One of the biggest lessons I needed to learn early on was that we can't control how others feel about us, but we can control how we feel about *them*. In this chapter, we're going to dredge up all the bullshit excuses you use to stop yourself from going after what you want. We're going to look at all the people you keep blaming – the ones you let control your emotional state – and show you how to take that power back.

It's time to take control of your life. It's time to take responsibility for your actions. It's time to have what you want and become the leader you know you can be.

Mindset

I've been immersed in the world of seduction and dating since 2007, but before I went to college, I lacked the necessary confidence. I had low self-esteem and I was holding on to negative reference points from my past. My earliest experiences with girls were at pre-school where I got bullied by girls so severely that I came home with cuts and bruises down my legs.

It got to the point that during primary school I began going home for lunch each day so I didn't have to experience the discomfort of interacting with people in the playground. That was before I started to take responsibility.

And as a teenager, I wasn't emotionally mature enough to deal with the comments people made about my height and my gangly look.

When I started college, I chose to position myself around the right people, moving myself away from any friends I felt were holding me back. I had inherited a lot of my friends from the all-boys school I had gone to, and a lot of these friends would hide their inadequacy with women behind drinking. Whenever I built up the courage to make a move, they had a lot of jealousy, and their obnoxious behaviour stymied my efforts.

They didn't want to push themselves to get outside of their comfort zone and go to the clubs where I knew we could find the hotter women. They wanted to stay small and remain in familiar areas.

But I knew I had a lot to learn, and I took it upon myself to find people who could mentor me. I chose to hang around with men who enjoyed meeting women, men who were open-minded to developing and improving this area of their life, men who wanted to have expereinces with women. Men who understood the "guy code".

These men would introduce each other as someone of value and were the type of guys who would even interact with women they didn't like just to support you. These men were unselfish, had charm and knew how to build on a conversation.

By being around these men and by reading books on dating, my mindset soon shifted from "go out and get laid" to "go out and study human behaviour". I would go out and just talk to people and try out different conversation techniques I'd read about. In a sense, these conversations became market research.

If something didn't go too well, I didn't beat myself up saying things like, "I'm shit" or "I suck". My critiques of myself were always positive and constructive, and that allowed me to move forward.

The key was to create positive reference points (more on this in the next chapter) and experiences I could learn from and build on. These experiences got me out of my head and into a mindset where I was less attached to outcome. I was simply learning what was possible.

Cowards in the Coffee Hut

It was 2007.

I was studying Motorsport Engineering at Brooklands College in Weybridge, and you can imagine how many women were on that course! If there was a girl at all, I wasn't stimulated by the way these women looked. So, my friends and I spent our lunch breaks trying to get close to the people on neighbouring courses, the ones a bit more populated with hot young girls, i.e. Civil Service.

Every day at lunchtime, I and a handful of the guys from the engineering course would head over to the on-campus coffee shop. When we arrived, we always saw the same group of girls secure on the sofa. Unfortunately, none of my friends nor I had an ounce of courage between us to actually go over to talk to them. We remained silent and those girls remained the elephant in the room.

As far as we were concerned, speaking to them was taboo. And I personally still had a great deal of anxiety about approaching women like that in the daytime.

I had no idea what to say and there was something that I couldn't quite put my finger on holding me back.

The Triumphant Hangover

One day, I had an experience that completely changed how I viewed social interactions with women and I discovered what it was that had been holding me back.

It was a Saturday afternoon, and I was hungover from the night before. Looking for something to do, a couple of us decided to head to the Oracle Shopping Centre in Reading.

I saw this girl as I was coming down the escalator: slightly tarty, tanned, brunette, tits pushed up with a push-up bra. At the time, my ideal girl was what I saw in magazines like *Max Power* or *FHM*, so I was pretty drawn to her, and since it had always been my fantasy to approach a woman in the daytime, I decided to approach her.

I looked at her first, she looked back. I smiled, she smiled. I went, *Fuck it, John. Just do it,* then found myself going over to say, "Hey, it's Johnny." I took down her number, had a bit of light conversation (nothing amazing), and before I knew it, we were dating.

I thought back to what had made that day different from all those days in the coffee hut and realized what it was. Ultimately, if you don't take the risk you don't get the reward.

---

*"It's **more** disrespectful to be so **respectful** that you don't show your intent"* – Johnny Cassell

---

Why You're Terrified of Approaching Women

I chose these two stories because they show two obviously contrasting situations: one where I hesitated, and one where I chose to do something.

So what was the difference? Why didn't I talk to the girls in the coffee hut?

It was because of *that* feeling.

You know the feeling I'm talking about – the one that lies in the pit of your stomach when you feel like there's something you want in front of you and you aren't taking action to get it. This can be a career opportunity, an attractive woman, or anything that seems like a risk. Most people call it "anxiety" or "nerves".

To me, anxiety and nerves are negative terms evoking fear. Instead of moving you forward toward your goal, they encouage you to retreat. You never get rid of *that* feeling, but you can take responsibility for choosing what label you put on it. The key is to reframe that feeling into something that promotes positive action. So when that feeling comes over me, I don't call it "anxiety" or "nerves"; I call it "excitement".

The reason I *did* talk to that girl in the shopping mall was because I was excited. Yes, I used being hungover as an excuse to approach her, but people framing their apprehension as "anxiety" would just as easily use "being hungover" as a reason not to approach. But I was excited enough in the moment that I didn't need to look for an excuse not to act.

The lesson here is that any reason you tell yourself for why you shouldn't do something is actually the reason why you *should*. Hungover? Approach. She's got headphones in? Make your move. She's on the phone? Head on over. She's with her mum or her friends? Go talk to her.

Any excuse you can think of should be your reason to act. It's all part of the story of how you met. And women love stories. She'll tell her friends "I was walking down the road. I had my headphones in and this guy just came and approached me," or, "I was walking with my mum. Can you believe it? And he came over and talked to me," or, "He was totally hungover

from the night before and he came over and struck up a conversation and we've been dating ever since".

Whatever excuse you used to use to stop yourself can be the story she keeps telling her friends.

Stop Acting Like a Princess

Life is not a fairy tale. We can't just sit and wait for something to fall into our lap. Neil Strauss, in his book, *The Game*, says:

"In life, people tend to wait for good things to come to them. And by waiting, they miss out. Usually, what you wish for doesn't fall in your lap; it falls somewhere nearby, and you have to recognise it, stand up, and put in the time and work it takes to get to it. This isn't because the universe is cruel. It's because the universe is smart. It has its own cat-string theory and knows we don't appreciate things that fall into our laps."

People keep telling us, "Don't worry. It will just happen. Someone will come along." Someone may come along, but it doesn't "just happen". It just doesn't.

Opportunity lands close, but if you're not awake or aware, and you don't have the skill set, then you're not going to recognise let alone capitalise on it. Fairy tales don't happen to us. It's up to us to create them.

Remember all those reasons you keep telling yourself for why you can't go talk to her? Jump forward and think about the stories she keeps telling her friends; *that's* the fairy tale. As crazy as the situation may be and as ridiculous as it may sound, the reasons for why you shouldn't do something are the exact reasons why you should.

Imagine your *ideal woman* sitting around a table with her girlfriends and them going around the table asking, "How did you meet your partner?"

"I met my partner at work. He's my boss. I was his secretary."

"Okay. What about you? How did you meet your partner?"

"I met him on Tinder."

"What about you?"

"I was introduced by a friend."

"How about you, '*ideal woman*'? How did you meet your partner?"

"I was at my lunch break one day and went out for a sandwich. This guy came right out of nowhere, told me how amazing I was and we've been dating ever since."

All the girls sitting around the table would look at that girl and think, "Fuck you, bitch. I want that story."

Everyone grew up the same way. Everyone was conditioned by all that Cinderella, Prince Charming crap. It's the story every woman wants, so use the ridiculousness of the situation to fuel your approach.

If You're Unhappy, You've Settled for Less than You Deserve

The majority of people settle for a mediocre life. Mediocrity is comfortable and it's safe, and for some people, that's enough.

If you've picked up this book, I'm guessing you're not one of those people. You're looking for more than mere contentment. You're looking for someone who has the right qualities – someone worthy of long-term investment.

But you need to take responsibility for finding what you want. If you're not finding your ideal mate, or not approaching them when you do find them, then you're stuck, and you have nobody to blame but yourself.

When you blame other people, you're not taking responsibility for your own growth and development and you're giving up your power to change things. In that moment of blaming, you are telling yourself, "There's nothing else I could've done."

But how are you going to grow if you're not taking responsibility for your actions?

In dating as in life, you can either be a proactive strategist or a passive, blaming victim. When we blame people, our problems stop being our fault. We are no longer constructively breaking down our mistakes and working at a solution. We are moving away from a strategy to achieve what we want, making us free to repeat the same mistakes over and over again.

Every chance you get, you should be asking, "How can I do better?" If you bring this mindset to every hurdle you face, you're going to move towards being a solution-based thinker.

Everything can be deconstructed and unpacked, and analysed. If something's not working, then it needs fixing. That includes yourself.

---

*"**Practise risk** in all areas of your life"*
– Johnny Cassell

Techniques:

Automatic Thinking

Whenever I used to go out and see someone who was particularly well-dressed, I had this impulsive response where I looked at the guy and thought, "What a tosser".

This knee-jerk negative response towards the GQ look started at an early age. It was a feeling I couldn't control – a reflex, or so I thought. I eventually realized what it really was: insecurity. At the time, I wasn't particularly confident in terms of the way I dressed and my personal image. So I was just reacting automatically to one of my weaknesses.

Automatic thinking is where, reacting to stimuli in our environment, we move automatically toward a positive or negative mindset.

When I started becoming aware of automatic thinking, I began catching my negative thoughts, and I started asking myself the following questions, "Why is he a tosser?", "Why is he a dick?".

Then I had a realisation.

"What is the opposite to this?" I thought. "What is the complete opposite reaction to seeing a guy like that?" Soon, I found myself going over to the guy, shaking his hand and saying, "Hi, it's Johnny. I just had to come over. You're the best-dressed guy in here today."

Soon I was sharing in all the positive attention he was getting because I was now seen as his friend, someone of "social value". I'll get to social value in Chapter Seven, but this is just one example of how you can reframe a situation by controlling your automatic thinking.

The key word here is *choose*. When an event occurs, rather than allowing yourself to go straight toward negative thinking or even positive thinking, I want you to remember that you can *choose*.

Let's go back to that same situation. A guy walks in looking well-dressed. This time I don't go negative. I don't go positive. Instead, I *choose* to think, "Is he a tosser?" or, "Am I going to go over there and do something about it?".

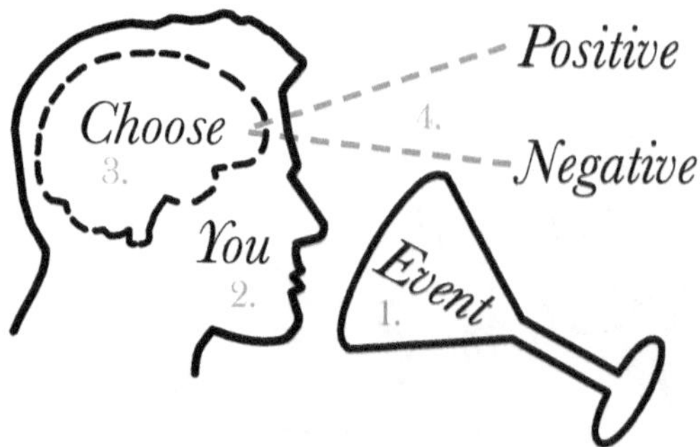

Whatever that certain situation is in your life that keeps on occurring, you are probably conscious of the way you typically respond. Automatic thinking is a pattern of thought, but patterns can be broken. From now on, instead of just reacting, I want you to *choose whether you're going to go negative or positive.* Ultimately, we want to flush out all the negative reactions. Negativity is exhausting and draining, and it doesn't help you reach your ideal reality.

Automatic thinking can come into play at other times, like when you see an attractive woman walking into the bar. Your automatic response might be something like, "Oh my God. She's fucking incredible. She's so hot." That may sound like a positive mindset, but what you're basically doing in that moment is putting her on a pedestal and moving yourself away from taking any action at all.

I recall the time when I was becoming aware of this way of thinking. I was at a friend's bar and this knockout walked in. I saw her in my peripheral vision, and I knew exactly how my friend would react.

Naturally he freaked out, "Oh my God. Johnny, Johnny, look, look, look at her."

This time I didn't play into his reaction. Instead, I decided to incorporate that little magic word: *choose*. As he carried on about how hot she was, I *chose* whether to elevate her or neutralise her. I thought to myself, "She's okay," and it allowed me to go over there and do something about it. I left that night with her number.

By slowing my automatic thinking and making a choice, I was able to reframe the situation. You can do the same thing, but first you have to **figure out what you automatically think**.

Exercise: How to Determine Your Automatic Thoughts

1. Imagine each of the following situations.
2. For each situation, write down your first reaction.

There are no right answers; the objective is simply to understand how you think. Focus on being true to yourself, and be honest with how you feel.

Situations:
- You spot a beautiful woman on the train. She's directly opposite you and you can't stop looking at her. Suddenly she looks up and smiles. *How do you react?*
- You walk into a bar and you see a guy who's wearing a very low cut top, has a fake tan and huge muscles. He's surrounded by women, and they're all laughing and smiling. *How do you react?*
- You're in a coffee shop. It's not busy and there are three baristas chatting behind the counter. You stand at the till for 30 seconds and catch the eye of one of the baristas. They look at you and then return to their conversation. *How do you react?*

Whatever you have written down are good examples of your automatic thinking. You don't need to do anything about it yet (that's what reframing is for), but once you've got the hang of recognising your automatic thinking, you can use the same technique when you're out and about.

Now that you've got a good idea of your typical reactions, it's time to *upgrade* your thinking by learning how to turn these situations into opportunities through the power of "reframing".

Reframing

Reframing is all about taking control of your perception. Literally, changing how you see the world. In the same way I

changed my perception of the guy dressed like a GQ model, I'm going to show you how you can remove your own fears and insecurities.

Here's a great exercise to practise with. I want you to **make a list of excuses** that you come up with when you see an attractive woman in the street or in any environment. For example:

- She's got her headphones in.
- She looks like she's in a rush.
- She's on the phone.
- She just went into that shop.
- She looked at you then looked away.
- She got in a car.
- She's with her mum.

Now make a list of all of the people you blame for limiting your success – the people you think hold you back. The list might include:

- Parents
- A bully
- Your boss
- Your ex-girlfriend
- Your friends.

Most likely, you're looking at these lists with a negative point of view. But the things you listed are all just excuses that prevent you from taking action.

Let's look at the first list: your excuses. What if you changed your perspective and saw these excuses as reasons for why you *should* approach? She's wearing her headphones? That's a great talking point! You could say, "I had to come over. I saw you had your headphones in and I just need to check if we had the same music taste." Or, "I don't normally do this and I see you've got your headphones in, but I thought, 'Fuck it, I'm gonna do it anyway'." Or, "I just found out I've got the superpower of guessing what song people are listening to and I just had to show it off."

The more ridiculous the excuse, the better, because remember what I said earlier, it adds to the fairy tale, the story they're going to tell their friends:

"He approached me when I was with my mum, and he instantly got my mum's approval because I was with her when he talked to me."

"I was with 10 of my friends. We were out shopping in London, and he came over and approached me."

Remember mindset and reframing? Instead of calling all these situations obstacles, call them hurdles. Each of the excuses you listed is a hurdle you just need to jump. Doing so will be a great display of confidence.

Now look at your second list: all the people you blame. That list can bring up a lot of anger and resentment. But you can reframe that too and realize you've got something to be thankful for. In their own way, these people have contributed to your progress in life.

For example, you may have a parental figure you feel oppressed you for a period of your life. But you can be thankful for them and that experience because it led to you learning independence or to you wanting to take action to develop this area of your life.

I feel everyone has a cage they need to escape to become who they are meant to be. Parents are a common cage, but it could also be an ex-partner – someone you're still harbouring bad thoughts about because they treated you badly. You need to reframe this. Look at the situation and be thankful for these

people helping you to realise what you are worth, and for showing you what kind of person you want to be with.

Back to the girl I met in the shopping mall. She became my girlfriend for two years, but she was still sleeping with her ex the whole time, and she never slept with me.

At the time I felt emasculated. It didn't feel like I was being my true, authentic self. Putting up with her behaviour for the "greater good" blinded me. My infatuation with her meant I was treading carefully and letting her get away with disrespectful behaviour because I was too scared of losing her. I hadn't had the experience of seducing a woman before and I was scared it might never happen again.

I put her physical looks on a pedestal and overlooked all her negatives. Today, I'm thankful she did that because, if she hadn't, I wouldn't have gone on this journey and discovered that I could claim my self-respect. If I had carried on with that relationship, it would have destroyed me.

Instead of holding a grudge against those people on your list, look at the value they have added to your life. Love and appreciate them for the ways in which they have helped you grow, and then cut them loose.

If you're trying to develop your confidence, and you're going out three or four nights a week, studying human behaviour, these are not the people to have around. You can still see them in social or family gatherings, but you need to surround yourself with people who build you up, not hold you back.

Exercise: Reframe the Blame

For this exercise you're going to need a sheet of A4, a pen, and some creativity.

1. Divide your sheet of A4 into two columns.
2. Label the columns "Excuse" and "Reason".
3. Write down all the excuses in the "Excuse" column.
4. In the "Reason" column, write down why each excuse is a *reason* to talk to someone.

Here's an example:

Excuse:	Reason:
She's with her friends	If she's with all her friends, they're having a great time and want to meet new people
She's got headphones in	We can easily connect through our shared love of music/podcasts
She's with her mum	I can use the fact that I've already met her mum to build comfort
She looks bored	She wants to meet someone that will make her day more exciting
She looked at you then looked away	I should make a joke about being so incredibly attractive that she had to force herself to take her eyes off me

With your list of reasons, you're building a bank of ideas and conversational openers to test out and use when you approach women. Only after you've tried out these reasons for approaching three to five times each, can you make the decision to change them or get rid of them.

Now we're going to look at the people you blame for limiting your success. Again, you'll need an A4 sheet of paper, a pen, and an objective mindset.

1. Divide your sheet of A4 into three columns.
2. Label the coloumns "Name", "Action", "Consequence".
3. Write down all the names of the people you feel have limited you in the "Name" column.
4. Write down the thing(s) they did that caused you to feel limited in the "Action" column.
5. Write down the positive outcome of that action in the "Consequence" column.

Here's what this looks like:

Name	Action	Consequence
Dad	Spent too much time at work and not enough time with me	I learned how to be independent and how to find my own source of fun
Richard (Boss)	Constantly belittled me at work and tried to "one-up" me all the time	I learned how to deal with bullies and stand-up for myself
Sylvia (Ex)	Cheated on me	I learned how to value myself and to not tolerate disrespectful actions

It's necessary to be objective in this exercise as your automatic thinking may still be caught up in negative emotional responses to these people. Remember that, whilst it was their action that inspired the consequence, it was *you* who made the decision to pursue it.

Building Your Dream Team

Here's another practical exercise that will help you take responsibility for your social prospects. Make a list of all the people you *want* to be around. **Make a list of all the people who you think can help you on your journey**.

What are the common traits of these people? What we're trying to do is build up some awareness by training your conscious mind to look for those traits when people come into your presence, so you can take responsibility and include them in your life.

Now, look at yourself. What are the areas you're weak in? Maybe it's physical fitness. Maybe you want to put on a few extra pounds of muscle or lose a few pounds of fat. Maybe you just want to get toned. Who is that person you can hit up to go to the gym with?

For me that person was Andy. When I was looking to improve my fitness, I would spend a lot more time with him. Andy was competing in the Olympics, and health and fitness was (and still is) a big part of his lifestyle. Spending more time with Andy helped me develop fitness routines, habits, and the discipline required to create the body I wanted.

This applies to your abilities with women as well. Maybe you realise you can spark up a great conversation with a woman, but you can't turn it sexual. Who on your list can? If it's nobody, then you need to find that person and add them to your list. Maybe you realise you can approach a woman in the evening, but you can't approach her in the day. You need to find someone who can demonstrate and give you advice about that.

What I'm talking about is actively working on your growth. That means keeping track of your "sticking points", writing them down and looking for people and methods that can help you overcome them.

Your list of people is there to help you get to the next stage in your life. Not only that, it is a list of sticking points, things you need to work on. Once you're aware of your weaknesses, you can remove yourself from being a blamer and start being accountable.

Exercise: Dream Team Creation

When you approach a challenge, you need to break it down into its key components and solve or fix each component one-by-one. When it comes to dating and seduction, that means thinking about all the areas where you know you could do better.

This may be components like: fashion, conversation, fitness, or emotional connection. Think about the person you'd most like to be like, and write that list.

1. Think of all the different characteristics you'd like to improve in yourself and not just with dating.
2. Write down each characteristic.
3. Next to each item, write down the name of someone who can help you in that area.
4. If you can't think of anyone who can help you, write down places where that kind of person might hang out, e.g. "Fitness – The Gym".

Here's a basic example that I created in my journal:

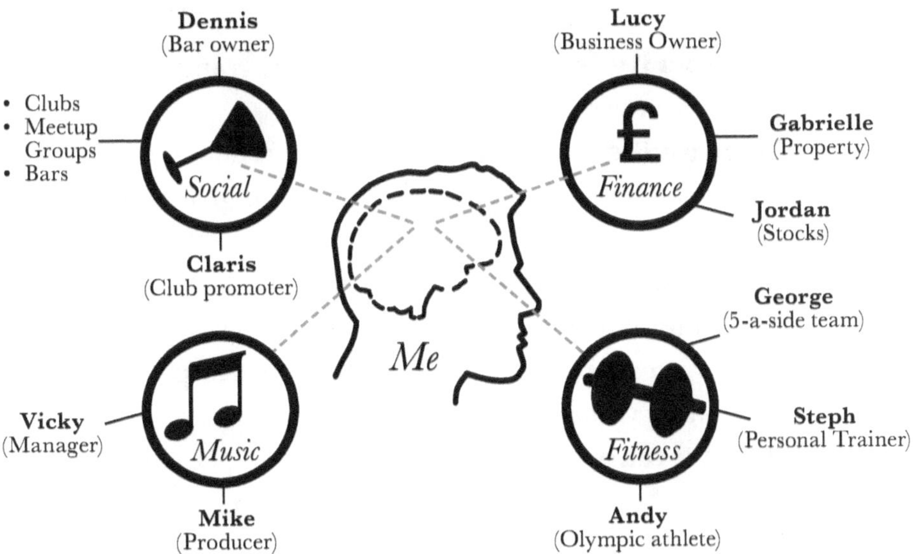

What you've created is a plan of action of who can help you succeed and what they can help you succeed with. The next stage is to contact each person and explore how the two of you can help each other.

Takeaways

Once you take responsibility for your life, you can start living the life you know you deserve, but you need to be the master of your own destiny and take charge.

When you allow external forces to influence how you feel internally, you lose your innate ability to shape your perceptions, outcomes, and emotional state. You are telling yourself, "I am not responsible."

In reality, you have complete control over your thoughts, your actions, and the types of people you spend time with. Until you understand that, you'll be stuck living the same mediocre life you've always led.

Here are the five key takeaways from this chapter:

1. **Mediocrity is your fault:** No one is going to *give* you the life you want; you need to *create* it.
2. **Stop giving away your power:** When you blame someone else for how you're feeling, you give away your power.
3. **Train your brain:** You need to be able to recognise your automatic thoughts, before you can change them.
4. **Focus on opportunity:** Find the positive potential in everything you do.
5. **Build a team:** Position yourself around people smarter than you in the areas you'd like to improve.

Chapter One: Case Study

Name: Vik

Profession: Optometrist

What areas of your dating world did Johnny work with you on?

I worked with Johnny on cold approaching, day and night. Conversation, making compliments and sexual escalation. Also worked on body language and my wardrobe.

How did working with Johnny on Taking Responsibility change your life?

It made me more aware of things that I never paid attention to before. An example of this is my wardrobe. Now I pay attention to what guys and girls are wearing. I am quick to give my opinion on things. Now I receive compliments about what I wear. I never had that before.

Which of the techniques that Johnny taught you do you still use on a regular basis?

I still use the element of surprise when I date or approach. To catch someone off guard, in a good way, is great. I also use body language techniques in business meetings.

How did working with Johnny help you outside of the dating world?

I would say wardrobe is a big one, and body language. Wearing the right clothes is hugely important when it comes to positioning yourself in business and in dating.

What was the most valuable lesson Johnny taught you?

He made me realise what my Achilles heel was. Sexual escalation. It took some time to realise this, but when we did, we specifically targeted it through role play.

For more resources and access to **'5 Seduction Secrets High-Class Women WISH you knew'**, head over to *www.JohnnyCassell.com/BookResources*

Self-Coaching

"You only really fail when you fail to do anything"
– Johnny Cassell

We should all be looking to get help and guidance in the areas of our lives where we need to grow. At the same time, we need to be doing the work ourselves. Relying on a coach is not enough to make real progress in anything. We need to coach ourselves.

If you're taking driving lessons, you can do your couple of lessons a week, but if you're not jumping in the car with an experienced adult in your own time and brushing up on those skills, then each lesson is going to feel like your first lesson because you haven't put the time in to learn on your own.

Self-coaching is a powerful tool because it helps you build positive reference points by becoming a more solution-based thinker actively looking for positive outcomes.

If you're like most people I coach, you might say, "Yes, I need you there because you push me."

That's fine.

I can take you to a stage you can't see in front of you because I've been there before, and I know what the next step is. At the same time, *you* need to be making approaches, working on your sticking points and trying out different variations of newly acquired techniques in your own time. Otherwise, you're going to use that external factor of a coach as a crutch.

Later in this chapter, I'm going to teach you two systems that will allow you to get to work straight away on self-coaching. The first system is three questions you need to be asking yourself every time you go into the field. The second system is the hurdle system – the language I use to describe your sticking points, making you aware of what's holding you back and giving you practical instant solutions if those hurdles come up again.

Story: The Lads' Guide to Going Home Alone

When I was first coming to grips with seduction dynamics, I went out mainly to get drunk with the lads with the faint hope of getting laid. We'd go to some commercial place with five or ten of us and check out the women standing at the bar next to us. But we wouldn't even know what to say to open the conversation.

We thought the girls were just going to land in our laps from some miracle. None of my friends had the balls to approach. We were comfortable in our own little circle, happy to just be chatting bullshit. Of course, I never went home with anyone because I was putting too much pressure on myself.

Later I subscribed to a new model of thinking, going out to meet fun and interesting people. That mental shift was important because it allowed me to go out and actually *meet fun and interesting people*, and then whatever happened after that would just be a fantastic addition.

During this phase, I grew more confident in building relationships from scratch, meeting strangers and people outside of my friendship circle. I became more aware of how my reality could be different, and I started splintering away from these guys and just coaching myself through the evening, analysing what I was doing and writing things down.

One particular evening, I approached this group of girls. The guys spotted me and started just launching ice cubes over at me. A couple of these ice cubes hit my head which was hilarious for my friends, but I was embarrassed. It was a perfect metaphor of how much of an obstruction these people were in terms of my growth.

Some would come up and actually try and make me look like a fool in front of these girls. Again, they would never approach girls on their own, but if it came to me approaching, they'd happily jump on the bandwagon and try and make me look like an idiot for their own gain.

I walked away from that group of women, frustated and pissed off that my "friends" were behaving in such childlike ways. It's important to build a social circle in which people are on the same page and have the same outlook. That's not to say I ditched these lads completely. I just positioned them into a different area of my life. These were great guys to have a laugh with, but they weren't necessarily going to be instrumental in terms of my success with meeting women.

Story: A Valentine's Holiday to... Swindon

Over time, I splintered away from my idiot friends, who were just caught up in that culture of going out and getting pissed. That's when I started getting traction.

I started seeing that I was meeting girls and having positive conversations with them. This was simply a function of practice. You can't go out that amount of times and not get bored of having the same conversations. And if you're getting bored, imagine how bored she is. You need to do what you can to better the conversation. When you do, there is no competition. You're ahead of the game.

After a time, I realized, "I'm on to something here."

At first, I didn't want to share this with anyone. I was very selfish with what I knew because, being a young kid, I was in a mindset of "I'm going to fuck *all* the girls". It was a pretty normal attitude to have, but it didn't last. Eventually I hit a ceiling, and I started to think it would be a lot more fun to share what I knew with someone else.

I looked in my friendship group, and though I was into the more commercial R&B scene, I picked out a friend, Louie, who was part of that Indie/Alternative scene. He shared the same mindset of wanting to improve himself and was a decent guy who could be trusted to not abuse the techniques I would teach him. I decided to take him out and mentor him. We dedicated five nights a week to going out, and at the end of those two years, he found his ideal woman.

James was the second guy I mentored, and he was a hybrid, who jumped between both scenes. We studied a lot of hypnotic language and NLP (Neuro-Linguistic Programming,

a communication style). I remember us just sitting at his house practising the language patterns on each other. We were sceptical ourselves to see if hypnotic language would even work. Both of us were straight, but we were actually turning each other on with the techniques we were using on each other.

One of my favourite memories was from Valentine's Day. At the time, James and I both chose to be single because we were both going on a seduction journey, but that Valentine's Day, it seemed like everyone was coupling off and doing romantic things with their loved ones.

I was like, "Fuck, what do we do? Are we just staying in? We need to capitalise on this opportunity!"

And that's exactly what we did, albeit with a holiday vibe.

When you're on holiday, you allow yourself to come out of your shell a little bit more and try new things. So I suggested we go down to the next town to liven things up.

We jumped in the car, sped down the motorway, listening to an audio guide on how to meet women, and getting pumped up. Ambitiously, we booked a hotel room, and when we went out, we were on fire. We approached every woman in every club we went to. We were even introducing different groups of people to each other.

I remember wearing some silly pink, fluffy headphones just as a talking point and by the end of the night, we both... came back empty handed.

But it wasn't about getting laid. This was a "field" trip.

At the end of the night, we sat down in the hotel and went through every single group approach we had done, discussed how we had behaved and critiqued each other. We didn't pull any punches. It's the attitude you need to have when you're going through a process like this.

When you're self-coaching, you need to analyse what you're doing and refine your behaviour to take you to the next step. But you can't see what you're doing and read your own behaviour when you're so far in. It takes someone else to come in and tell you what you're doing wrong. So that's what we did, and we didn't emotionally respond to the criticism because it was what we wanted, and it strengthened the dynamic between us.

"The more poeple you interact with. The more familiar you become in social situations." – Johnny Cassell

Seduction is all about the D...edication

To break out of that "I'm going out to get drunk" mindset and move toward the "I'm going out to meet interesting people" mindset takes a lot of discipline and dedication. You've got to break the habit of what you associate with going out.

You might associate going out with blowing your month's pay cheque, getting absolutely pissed, or getting a tattoo at whatever hour in the morning. But if you want your evenings to get better, you cannot go on with that kind of behaviour. You need discipline.

Here is a new rule: **if you're going to drink, just have two drinks.**

Just two.

When you're learning a new habit or a new skill, you want to be awake. You want to be aware of all of the new knowledge you are consuming and how your actions affect the

environment around you. Once you master that, then you can allow yourself to maybe have a few more drinks and let go a little bit.

At the first stage, you need to be disciplined enough just to go out there and remember your night. Realistically, if you're going out five nights a week, and you're drinking every night, you're going to be an alcoholic.

Five nights a week?! you ask. Yes.

When it comes to going out this much, it's so easy just to have that "I can't be bothered" attitude. If you "can't be bothered", it's that attitude that's going to leave you with you a woman who doesn't tick your boxes. An incredible woman is not going to put up with your lousy "can't be bothered" attitude. You need to be willing to go out more.

And it starts now. Make the commitment of going out five nights a week. Make the commitment to approach five women during the day, *every day*. Make the commitment to be a better version of yourself.

You Can't Read the Label from the Inside

In my Valentine's story, I spoke about how we are bad at perceiving ourselves from the inside. There are things we do that we're not conscious of because we can't see them.

Body language is a perfect example. You need someone to tell you how you're standing, or how you're coming across, or how you're behaving. It might be that you're so immersed in your own way of being that you haven't thought about it in any other way. You need someone to give you that different perspective. By looking at yourself objectively, with outside eyes, you're allowing yourself to improve.

If you don't allow someone to critique you, then you're chosing to remain ignorant and you're not being forward-thinking. You are great because of the influences you've had in your life, so allow the friends you admire to influence you for the better.

I saw a video on YouTube (www.johnnycassell.com/bookresources) about behaviour from Charlie Munger (Warren Buffet's business partner). In it, he said, "If you want to master anything, you got to watch one, do one and teach one." This resonated with me because I related it back to my journey. I started thinking about all the people I worked with, and why I'm so successful. It's *exactly* the same in the dating world.

Perhaps you are in a bar (or bingewatching YouTube) and you watch someone who is a bit more confident with women. You see them making their approach. You see how well the women respond to them. It's inspiring. And it gives you positive references (more on positive references next chapter).

But you can't just sit there and "watch one" all the time. There comes a point where you must actually "do one". You need to do it yourself so you get the positive reference rather than it just remaining a fantasy. "Doing one" means going out in the evening or the daytime, and *actually* approaching someone.

That brings me to teaching. If you want to accelerate your progress, there is no better way than sharing. Don't be selfish like I was in the early days. Just teach someone who is in need of this skill set in their life.

When you teach, you're constantly reinforcing and honing your skills. My best teaching content comes when I have been asked the best questions because I have to dig deep. If you're

constantly challenged, then you're constantly reminded of your own knowledge, and you gain a deeper understanding of *how* and *why* it works.

"When you say, 'I can't' you miss every opportunity. 'How can I?' opens up a world of possibilities"
– Johnny Cassell

Techniques:

Track Your Growth

A tough aspect of learning the dynamics of seduction is that it's difficult to see progress and, because dating feels so personal, it's easy to take a bad interaction poorly. To negate this, and track my progress, I used a pocket journal.

In this pocket journal, I would record my successes. If I'd gone out that night and qualified someone, I'd go home and put that in the diary. If I'd gone out and spoken to a certain category of women, I'd go back to the diary and I'd write that down. When I got laid, I'd write that down.

Whatever success, however big or small (everyone's level of success is different), you need to record it.

I look at another time in my life where I didn't track my success. I started doubting myself. I started getting frustrated. I grew depressed about not nailing the property investment area of my life. In reality, I was doing just fine. I just hit a new

ceiling and I needed one last thing to punch through. But because I wasn't recording all my successes, I was just focusing on what I hadn't gotten rather than what I already had.

If you don't record your successes, you are only going to be focusing on the things you haven't gotten rather than appreciate the things you've already done.

You're always going to have that voice in your head telling you why you're shit. That's normal. Your journal of success will help you turn the volume of that voice down and listen to your logical side.

Check out more on diaries at www.johnnycassell.com/book resources.

Exercise: Power Pocket Journal

Here's what you need to do. Go now and get yourself a pocket journal and a pen to write with.

For me, the best pocket journal to get is the *Aspinal of London Refillable Pocket Notebook*. It uses A7 sized pages, feels amazing to write in, will keep your notes safe, *and* is refillable. Now, my recommendations for the notepad are just that, recommendations. Any pocket-sized journal and pen will do.

To get into the habit, each night do the following:

1. Write the date on the page.
2. Write down three things you feel you did well that day.

Start a new page for each day. Remember, this is a reference book for you to chart your successes. When you cram all your achievements together, it makes it difficult to track your progress as reading how far you've come becomes a chore. Breaking up your journal by day like this will help you to more clearly see your progress.

The Three Questions System

Whether you go to a bar, a party, a charity event, a brunch, or someone's birthday, after every night or every day, when you get back home, you need to ask yourself three questions:

- What did I do?
- What went well?
- What will I do better next time?

These are the same three questions I and my wing-men use and the questions I ask my students. These questions are so powerful because they urge you to constructively critique your actions and understanding of seduction dynamics.

Look at the questions. They're all positive. They're all forward-thinking. They're not condescending, telling you how shit you are or why you didn't ask x, y, z. They're not looking for answers as to why you *didn't* do something.

Instead, the questions look for answers as to how you can improve. That is the mindset you need to take to your journey. That is the structure you need to stick to. *Whatever* area you're focusing on, ask yourself those three questions.

Here's an example of how I use this technique with a client.

What did I do?

Yesterday, a client, Andrius, approached a blonde Russian girl on the high-steet.

What went well?
- Able to make her stop.
- Able to capture her attention for two minutes.
- She was receptive.

What will I do better next time?
- Run back in and go for the number.
- Enter the interaction with more energy.
- Take one step back from her physically.

As you're probably already thinking, this isn't something you can apply just to your dating life. This is something you can apply in any area of your life where you want to succeed.

I use this when I'm making content, for example:

What did I do?
Made a promotional video showing guys how to approach women.

What went well?
The audio sounds good.
- The humour is there.
- The presentation is great.

What will I do better next time?
- Change the format to capture their attention instantly.
- Talk to someone who can help me with my lighting.
- Upgrade my camera equipment.

By asking ourselves these three questions, we positively critique and pump logic into any given situation, thus teaching ourselves to become more solution-based. Similarly, by looking objectively at the situation and removing our emotional attachment to the outcome, we can observe each interaction and find better conclusions.

The Hurdle System

The Hurdle System is something I came up with, and it was designed with the notion in mind that women test you.

Women test you all the time, but they're not doing it for the reason you may think. They're testing you for your character. Women may behave in such a way to see if you're a guy that's got the minerals, or if you're just another wimp to throw on the pile.

Imagine you approach a woman, and imagine you're wearing some fancy little pocket square. She looks at you and says, "Nice pocket square. Are you gay?"

For a while, I had no comeback for that. The first time it happened, I was experimenting with flamboyance, and I may have come across as a bit camp for her. But at the time, I responded emotionally to her comment, not logically, and I showed her I was nervous and uncertain. So I went home and thought what two things I could say if that ever came up again.

I opened my notepad and drew a line, down the centre. Then I drew five or six "hurdles" on this line to visualize the obstacles in my path. Next to the first hurdle, I wrote, "Are you gay?" Then I came up with two responses: "I can only suggest you're complimenting me on the way I dress" and "I'm Omnivorous, actually".

Now if I put myself back in the field and that happens again, I'm ready with a response, and I'm going to make an impact because there's no way she is expecting a response like that. She is expecting me to trip up and mumble.

I call these kinds of comments or questions women give hurdles, because if you think of a hurdle, you think of something you're going to get over. Alternatively, you could call them speed bumps, just a little bump in the road en route to your goal.

You can use this system for everything. You can use it for conversation. You can use it for eye communication. You might struggle to approach in the daytime, or to approach women in coffee shops. Maybe you can't sexually escalate, or you can't build intimacy in conversation.

Your sticking points are going to be very diverse, but the idea is, if you think of that straight line moving forward and the hurdles as mere speed bumps on the way to your destination, you're in the right mindset. At first, you'll run into a ton of hurdles, but as you develop, you'll find the frequency decreases. You're becoming a solution-based thinker as opposed to someone who keeps getting stuck.

Takeaways

To be an effective self-coach, remember:

1. **Discipline yourself**: "Going out" is no longer about drinking; it's about observing social interactions and testing new techniques.
2. **Watch, Do, Teach**: Once you've read about the techniques in this book, go out and perform them in the real world. Once you've performed them a few times, teach someone else.
3. **Get a pocket diary:** Write down every "win". It doesn't matter how "small" you think it is.
4. **Ask yourself the three questions:** What did I do? What went well? What can I improve for next time?
5. **Build a Hurdle System:** For any obstacle you've run into, write down two solutions, then test them in the field.

Chapter Two: Case Study

Name: Dean
Age: 37
Profession: Property Developer

What areas of your dating world did Johnny work with you on?

Mainly the initial approach, the communication, how to feel comfortable, how to be relaxed and how to be receptive to a woman's signs of attraction.

How did working with Johnny on Self-coaching points change your life?

Life-changing, it's all mindset. It completely changes how you approach any relationship, friends, colleagues, and especially anyone you're attracted to. You need to get into a certain mindset to get confident and comfortable enough to create something where it didn't exist before. My perception has completely changed from working with Johnny.

Which of the techniques that Johnny taught you do you still use on a regular basis?

Going back to a frame of reference, to look at the positives, and to understand that you either win or you don't do it. There's no rejection or failure, there's just you and simply going out and presenting yourself to a woman is a victory in itself.

When you get into that mindset, it doesn't matter what happens. The end result will happen regardless. It's about getting out of your comfort zone and exploring different relationships, and different approaches. You don't look for the guarantee end result, but anything you do is simply about getting further or doing better than you did before.

How did working with Johnny help you outside of the dating world?

We look at dating because that's an obvious application, but really all the things he teaches is about bettering your own life. It's about looking at where your positives are and accentuating them using the tools that Johnny teaches you.

It's about relating to previous successes and channelling that happiness and prior achievement and pushing it into each interaction.

What was the most valuable lesson Johnny taught you?

There is no rejection. The victory is in getting outside your comfort zone. Focus on putting yourself in the position of discomfort and you'll get what you want.

For access to more exclusive techniques and the **'5 Seduction Secrets High-Class Women Wish You Knew'**, *www.JohnnyCassell.com/BookResources*

CHAPTER THREE:
Positive & Negative Reference Points

"Action breeds confidence and courage, inaction breeds doubt and fear" – Dale Carnegie

When an event happens in our lives, we make a choice. We choose to approach it using either a negative reference point or a positive reference point. Generally, we are wired to go negative.

We do this because that's the way we were conditioned to respond. We're conditioned by nature to recognise the things we don't have, the things we're not good at. We're not programmed to bank the positive reference points and reach for them in moments of insecurity.

Positive reference points, on the other hand, help us to construct a new reality. You may have the confidence to do everyday tasks at work because you have the positive reference of being able to do them on a day-to-day basis, but you need to build those positive reference points into other areas of your life.

In the last chapter, we spoke about the benefits of recording your successes in that little pocket journal. Another benefit of this is giving you a bank of positive reference points, so that, when you are in a situation where you need to call upon your past success, you have all the positive reference points you need.

When you ask women what they find attractive, they say "confidence". But that doesn't really help us. If we unpack that and look at what they actually mean, what they mean is they appreciate a man who comes from a place of certainty. How we get to that place is by having a collection of positive reference points. Positive reference points give you confidence, thereby making you attractive.

Using the reframing techniques in Chapter One, we helped you turn your negative reference points into constructive positive reference points. In this chapter, I'll share how to collect even more positive reference points, how to move into a place of certainty, and how to completely adopt the certainty mindset.

Story: Berkshire's Very Own Mike Tyson (...sort of)

Boxing was a sport I inherited from my father. I got into it at a very young age. I would always be dancing around the living room with boxing gloves on my hands, throwing punches and training with my dad. Once I was of age, I went down to the gym to train with him. It took me years to reach the right level of fitness.

Boxing is something everyone into self-development needs to experience. Getting in the ring with an opponent, throwing punches, taking a punch: no one's going to jump in and help you. It takes a lot of courage. I respect anyone who takes up such a sport.

For me, it was my first experience with training myself to take more risks in my life.

There's a certain feeling that goes through your body when your trainer shouts out to the entire boxing gym, "Who's sparring tonight?" If you give yourself time to talk yourself out of it, then you'll do the same thing when you see that beautiful woman on the street. You need to train yourself to take action and step out of your comfort zone.

So every time my trainer would say, "Who's sparring tonight?" I'd make sure I was always one of the first people to speak up. I wanted to be certain I was always ready to go.

In *all* contact sports, you *always* need to be ready.

Promoters know how flaky giving fights can be. An opponent might not make weight. Someone could chicken out or not train hard enough. There's so many variables when it comes to matchups that you never really know when you're going to get a fight, so you just have to be fit. You have to be ready when your trainer comes to you one day and says, "Listen, I got a fight for you in two weeks."

For my first fight, I trained extremely hard. Every night, if I wasn't at the gym, I was out putting miles in on the road.

I won.

I knocked him out in the second round, and it was an amazing feeling. After that, I was told I was going to get a fight every week, but that didn't happen. Things cooled down and months passed.

Then one day, my trainer tells me, "We got you a fight in two weeks."

I started questioning myself. "Have I been running as much as before? Have I done enough rounds sparring? Have I been practising my technique as much as I should be?"

I had the fight, and I lost.

Even though I trained extremely hard, I doubted that I had trained as hard as before, and I allowed that negative internal voice to deter me from any chance of winning.

I didn't get hurt or anything like that. I just lost on points. But in truth, I didn't lose the fight in the ring. I lost it outside. I lost it the moment I started doubting myself on how hard I had trained.

If we move this back into the arena of meeting women, women do not buy into hesitation. Your doubtful mind communicates to them, "I'm not secure in myself. How the hell can I offer you security?"

Story: The Nervous Olympian

Back in school, I had a friend who always missed the register. He would do a half day here and there because the one thing he always put first was kayaking. The guy was in phenomenal shape. He was incredibly disciplined and committed to his training, and soon reached an elite level, competing for the Olympics.

I was spending more and more time with this guy because I had chosen to be around people who strive for high levels of success. One day, I pulled him aside and said, "Listen, I want to know what your sports psychologist teaches you." I thought whatever came out of the conversation would only be beneficial for my clients.

He described to me how the mind is split up into two different hemispheres. You've got the irrational side, which is

described as the chimp brain, and the logical side, which is described as the human brain. He was making reference to Steve Peters' book *The Chimp Paradox* (a must read).

Thus, he told me, we need to come up with responses to manage the mind.

"Johnny, you know how long I've been training. You know how hard I've trained. You know how it's been a big part of my life. Would you believe that when I'm on a start line, I have these voices in my head that tell me, 'I'm shit. I can't do this'?"

An *Olympic athlete* was telling me this.

"You'll never learn how to get rid of it," he continued, "but what we've been taught is how to turn the volume of that down." This is when he shared with me something he called his "A-grade responses".

"It's the logical response to the irrational self-talk," he explained. "I remind myself of the time I held up the trophy in the Nationals. I remind myself of how long I've been training. I visualize how many trophies I've got at home in my cabinet. That's enough to put me back in focus. That's what pushes me across the line. I'd go as far to say, it's the difference between me being a winner or a loser."

That last part really resonated with me because, when I reference areas of my own life, like that boxing story, he's totally right.

I didn't manage my mind.

I let my mind fill with doubt, and I didn't address that scared voice with logic.

"All women want to be hit on. They just want it to be done right." – Johnny Cassell

---

Answering the Call of the Positive

When my Olympian friend talked about "A-grade responses", he was basically talking about positive reference points.

When it comes to seduction, I've accumulated a vast wealth of positive reference points. I feel like I can now act with certainty at all times because I've been in thousands of seduction environments and prevailed in the most extreme situations.

Once, I went out with a journalist who was notorious for writing negative columns about everyone. He wanted to see what we could do, so when I took him out, he would look at the women, click his fingers and say, "That one, that one, that one," telling me to approach.

There's a lot of pressure when you're coaching someone because you have to perform and you have to show them the ropes. But, when it's a journalist who only writes about bullshit, then the stakes are a lot higher. As the night wore on, I approached this woman who was in a birthday group of thirty, spread over two tables. I worked the group, pulled the journalist in and sat him next to me. Then I leaned over him, pulled the girl in and got her number. He saw the number go in my phone and he could not deny that I'd sealed the deal.

The next girl he picked out was this girl dancing intimately with this other guy most of the night. You could assume they were romantically involved, but I had to perform like a dancing monkey for that journalist, so, yes, I was able to get that girl's number as well.

The night was a complete success; unfortunately, nobody ever read about it. The journalist spiked the article because there was nothing negative to write. I held onto that positive reference point for years.

I have other positive reference points: dating models, CEOs, and TV personalities.

Whatever you choose as your positive reference points, however big or small, it's important to keep them close in your mind, because if you don't focus on building these up, you are going to focus on the negative, and that's a road you don't want to go down.

For example, you could focus on the time you approached someone and it didn't really go in your favour, or call upon a reference point for when you got bullied at school and how it is a metaphor for your relationship with women. But take it from me, as someone who has struck out with women and did get severely bullied at school (by girls), using positive reference points is a much better way to go.

Perception vs. Reality

When you're about to take action, your mind is either going to flick over to irrational thinking or logical thinking. As my friend (and Steve Peters) says, "It's the chimp or it's the human."

The chimp exists because you are calling upon your negative reference points. It's the irrational voice in your head telling you something can't be done. How you turn that volume down is by calling upon the human brain, the logical side, the positive reference points. You have to be aware of the way your mind works and use it to your advantage.

Having positive reference points will benefit not only your conversation, but also the way you conduct yourself as a whole. If you choose to come from a place of hesitance and doubt, then that is going to be evident in the things you say, in the tone you use when you speak, and how you carry yourself physically.

Your reference points carry through everything you do.

Women are looking to be led onto the path of seduction, and I feel it's our duty in society to oblige them. I'm all for empowerment of women and women taking more powerful roles in our society. I think it's an incredible sign of how far we've come over the years. But that has nothing to do with seduction. As men, it's still our duty to lead women into that seductive place. And if you are not coming from a place of certainty, you are demonstrating your inability to lead her to that place.

Positive reference points will enable you to act on things you once thought were risks, and to model successful behaviour from the past.

Think about basic conversation and how small changes make huge differences in how information is received. A simple request such as "May I have some water?" carries a polite tone. However, "I would like some water", although the exact same message, conveys a tone of power and, if incorrectly calibrated, arrogance.

Physical behaviour is a big part of this. Human beings are great at telling how someone is feeling simply by looking at their body language. If you see someone on the train, fidgeting, constantly rubbing their hands, and compulsively looking around, you instantly make an assumption about what's going on in their head. Now imagine someone sitting on the train: they are still with one leg resting on the other and their arm spread across the back on the chair next to them. What do you think *they* are thinking and feeling?

Unless trained otherwise, we humans are terrible at hiding our feelings. By keeping positive reference points in your mind, you transfer that certainty into your speaking patterns, your body language, and how you make others feel around you.

"If you're not around women, you're not learning about women." – Johnny Cassell

Techniques:

Pocket Journal – Part Two

When I had the pocket journal, I put it by my bedside table and added to it every night. I would add anything that was a conversation piece – that would build intimacy in any way. And I wrote down anything that was an example of me moving in the direction of progress and success.

I would also add in parties I was attending and new social groups I'd penetrated. I would even add things unrelated to dating, for example, if I'd charmed the barista at Pret a Manger and they'd given me a free coffee, or beaten a personal best at the gym.

You're of course going to get those nights when you come home and you feel like you haven't performed as well as the previous night. That's fine. The journal is exactly for those times when you go back home and in your mind, you are questioning yourself and your abilities. Your journal will give you the opportunity to answer back to your irrational mind because suddenly you will have hard evidence staring you in the face confirming why you are fucking awesome.

Like with the Three Questions System, you can use the pocket journal in other areas of your life. With my property investing I didn't use this technique and I was filling my head with doubt and self-pity. The moment I started journaling and reflecting upon my successes in this area was the moment I started moving forward in a more constructive manner.

What you choose to write down is up to you. No one's journal should look the same, but here are some moments when you might want to write:

- If you've discovered a new sticking point
- If you've found a solution to an old hurdle
- If you've found a new social group to play in
- If you've made a significant commitment
- If you've started meeting more attractive women.

Whatever it is, just keep on building and building this house of awesomeness in your journal.

Grade A Response Building

Think of all the things that give you that "nervous" feeling (and remember that feeling is now labelled "excitement"). **Write them down** in your pocket journal, and under each, include three bullet points.

We're going to scour your brain for three Grade A Responses to each of the imagined situations that fill you with "excitement".

I completely understand some of these situations you've written down may be situations that are completely new to you. So we're going to get creative.

Here's an example I did with one of my clients who was a 26-year-old virgin:

Situation: *"Having sex with a woman for the first time"*

Response 1: "When I had my first day at work I was incredibly nervous, but my colleagues treated me with respect and helped me with the tasks I didn't know how to do."

Response 2: "When I went skiing for the first time, I read three books on skiing before I went on the holiday. I used the knowledge from the books and quickly advanced from the "beginner" class to the "intermediate" class."

Response 3: "When I was 15, I was making out with a girl and I asked her what she liked about kissing. She told me that she'd never been asked that before and showed me how to kiss better."

The reference points we came up with were based around him going into a new environment unprepared, asking for help, and excelling doing something he'd never done before.

Alright, now it's your turn. **Look at your list** and come up with your own responses.

1. Turn to a blank page in your journal.
2. Write the situation that gives you that excited feeling at the top of the page.
3. Think of three Grade A Responses to similar situations.

It's important you frame these situations in an objective manner. For example, if approaching women gives you that feeling of excitement, think about what you're actually doing: *starting a conversation*. From there, write down three times that you've started a successful conversation.

In writing your own responses, look at the particular aspects of the situation that cause you excitement and find positive reference points in your life that demonstrate you can successfully deal with similar situations but in a different context.

"But I don't have any positive reference points."

Ever so often I meet someone who is in such a negative place they simply don't believe they have *any* positive reference points.

I call bullshit.

Everyone I've worked with including myself has positive reference points inside them. Once you find one (and you can always find one), the rest will bubble to the surface.

It may be that a girl asked to dance with you. It may be that you made a girl laugh when you told a joke. It could be *anything*. *Any* positive memory or experience you've had with a woman needs to be your default expectation for how an interaction is going to go.

Remember, you need to build yourself up in stages. Don't go into this exercise and think about what you *haven't* done. I've worked with high-net worth individuals who have never been kissed. I've worked with ultra-charming music producers who have never had sex. I've worked with super-fit personal trainers who have never had a proper conversation with a woman.

No matter where you're at on your journey, you need to build on the previous step. If you're learning how to approach women, I want you to remember three times when you introduced yourself and they instantly smiled. If you're learning how to get phone numbers, I want you to remember three conversations where you felt positivity radiating from the woman on the other end of the line. If you're getting dates and learning how to get laid, I want you to remember all the times the woman texted you, thanking you for taking them out.

Failing that, if you're still struggling to find your first positive reference point, I have one for you. Your first positive reference point was you taking action and picking up this book.

You have taken a concrete step to better your life. From that, you can take more steps and keep snowballing your reference points as you go deeper and deeper into taking more risks.

Takeaways

Remember:

1. **You'll never completely get rid of fear:** Your brain is designed to avoid the "pain" of fear by grabbing onto negative reference points. Don't listen.
2. **Perception is reality:** However you feel on the inside is what will show on the outside.
3. **You already have a positive reference:** You have plenty of positive past experiences to bank on. And if not, you've made a choice to better yourself by reading this book.
4. **Power-up your Pocket Diary:** Write down any positive reference points you have, and I mean *any*. Anything that made you feel amazing or gave you that feeling of accomplishment.
5. **Brainstorm three Grade A Responses:** Think of five situations that give you a huge level of "excitement" and write three Grade A Responses for each.

Chapter Three: Case Study

Name: Lex
Age: 28
Profession: Accountant

What areas of your dating world did Johnny work with you on?

Johnny shared a lot of content with me about how to develop interactions and how to connect with people. What's great about working with Johnny is that he forces you to apply the things that he teaches you in an environment that's out of your comfort zone.

Having him there to push me and nudge me makes the coaching really valuable.

How did working with Johnny on Positive and Negative Reference points change your life?

Johnny's given me a lot of confidence with actually going out and meeting random strangers, whereas previously I would've had some self-doubt about how they perceive me.

Now that I've gotten over that fear and that doubt, I'm free to give people value when I meet them and go out and create valuable relationships. Those connections have allowed me to get to know people and build my social circle.

Which of the techniques that Johnny taught you do you still use on a regular basis?

Being direct. People don't really know what I'm getting at and the conversation just trails off. Now I just state my intentions, it's a little scary but it yields quicker results.

How did working with Johnny help you outside of the dating world?

Now I can just go up to people and say, "You seem really interesting, let's have a chat and see how we can help each other".

In the business world this has been a hugely valuable skill to have as it has helped me to build my network.

What was the most valuable lesson Johnny taught you?

Just go for it. Apply all the knowledge you get. Once you actually test out and apply your knowledge you quickly see what works and what doesn't.

To learn more about constructing your Elite Seduction lifestyle, head over to *www.JohnnyCassell.com/BookResources*, where you'll find exclusive techniques and access to the **'5 Seduction Secrets High-Class Women Wish You Knew'.**

CHAPTER FOUR:
Body Language &
Spatial Awareness

"The conversation starts before you've even opened your mouth" – Johnny Cassell

---

The most common question I get from my clients is "What should I say to a woman?". But they are missing the point. Seduction has very little to do with what you say. The most important part of seduction (and communication) comes through body language. Poor body language is devastating and why excellent conversationalists can be perceived as "creepy" or "weird".

How you hold yourself is a reflection of what you're thinking. If you think you're worthless, then your body is going to communicate that to everyone around you, so you need to change your thoughts so you can change what you're projecting. I'm going to say that again:

Change your thoughts, change your perception, and how you're perceived.

This is why having positive reference points is so important in the world of seduction.

Spatial awareness is also important.

Spatial awareness means having consideration for your subject, your guests, and your friends. Imagine a circle on the floor, being drawn around the person in front of you. The closer you move to that circle, the more intimate things become. If you move into that circle, it becomes very intimate.

You want to move in the direction of intimacy, but if you push intimacy too quickly, or too forcefully, then you're going to get the reverse of what you want. It sounds counterintuitive, but you need to be standing *outside* of that person's circle.

I have a rule. When you approach someone you're talking to for the first time, remain at arm's length. There's no need to be so close to someone when you're talking to them. If you haven't spotted the cues that invite you into their space, then you are invading that space, and for your subject, it can be extremely intimidating.

In this chapter, I'm going to give you all of the know-how on how to respect people's space, how to be invited into their space, how to correct your body language so you can project your true, confident self, and how to walk through any environment and communicate to people non-verbally that you're interested in them.

I also will show you how you can spot the subtle cues women give to demonstrate their interest in you (in case you missed them already).

Story: From Gangly to Gorgeous

I have a condition called *pectus excavatum*. It's where my sternum goes inward instead of staying out. As a child, I hated getting changed in front of other people, and I was always the guy who had an excuse as to why he couldn't go swimming.

On top of that, I was always tall. I only realized the advantage of that many years later. But throughout my early years, I was always arching my back to shorten my stature. My head would hang over my chest, my shoulders would round inward, and I would slouch to accommodate shorter people.

I had terrible body language, and because of it, people could clearly see I wasn't a confident person. In order to change that perception, I became more conscious of how I was holding myself. I made sure to stand in a strong position with my feet shoulder-width apart. When I exercised at the gym, I made sure to do the necessary stretches to ensure I was standing up straight. I would stand in front of the mirror and practise, shoulders back, head at 45 degrees, feet shoulder-width apart and smile at myself. Once I learned how to stand properly and became more aware of my posture, I started attracting more high-calibre women.

Eventually I was able to pass this knowledge on to others. The first was my friend Rachel. When all my friends went to university, I had no one to go out with, so I invited her out.

"Rachel," I said, "come round next week. Bring a bottle of wine. Let's go out and meet fun, interesting people." What this girl didn't realize was she was signing up to be my wing-girl.

We created a fun environment and it turned into a fruitful friendship for many years. But early on, I could tell Rachel was hurting. Whenever I took her out with me, she looked like an

animal that had been wounded by a pellet gun. She was still suffering heartache over a guy she was lusting after. He would treat her terribly. They would have a one-night stand here and there, but nothing more. Because of that, she lacked a lot of self-confidence.

She was a lovely girl, with a ton of potential. I told her as much. But her body language reflected what was going on in her head. She often sat hunched with her chin scrunched over her neck.

After going out with me, Rachel got rid of her hunch, began smiling more, stood taller, pushed back her chest, and elongated her spine. Her change in body language and my encouragement and advice helped her build her confidence with men, and she became ten times as compelling to be around.

This once again demonstrates the power of teaching others. Not only did things improve for Rachel, but it was also great for me because people were looking at me thinking, "Oh, who's he? How is he out with a girl like that? What's the story with those two?"

From making subtle changes to our body language, Rachel and I matched our outward appearance with our inner awesomeness. All we needed to do was smile more and stand taller.

Until you focus on your body language, you may not be aware of the subtle sub-communications you're giving off. But the way you present yourself physically will affect what people perceive of you and your story before you even open your mouth.

"Unconsciously imply you already have a girlfriend. Don't go out there wanting and needing. Everyone can smell neediness." – Johnny Cassell

Picking Up Girls Like a Mime

A lot of energy gets wasted when you don't know what to do with your body. A lot of people get a bit fidgety. They fiddle with shirt buttons. They scratch their hair. They do these things because they feel uncomfortable, and they don't know what to do with that energy. But when you become aware of this and ground yourself more, you present a strong figure.

When I focus on making my body language "correct", my mind becomes less busy. I become more grounded, and that preserves my energy for conversation. To ground myself, I imagine myself looking in the mirror and becoming mindful of my posture. After all, the body is a reflection of what's going on in the mind.

It's extremely alluring for people to be around someone who is grounded. Everyone has some level of social anxiety, so for someone to stand there and feel perfectly comfortable in their own skin, communicates a huge amount without them even saying anything.

Non-verbal seduction is my favourite! These situations can be the most exciting because they require a higher level of awareness and intelligence, and in these scenarios, it's as if you and your partner have a secret language.

One night, I was out with a client in a bar. We got a table and sat down for a drink and a few light bites. I deliberately picked that particular table because I could hit eye-contact with someone as soon as they came in.

After a few minutes, this girl comes in with her friends, and *as soon* as she walks in, we throw eyes at each other. Once she settles in at her own table, I slowly move my head out of her line of sight.

From there, I play on and off it all night. I make eye contact and then look away. She does the same. She moves towards her friends and I talk to my friend. Each time, I move my head slowly to look at her. (That's the key to all body language: *slow everything down*. We'll talk more about that later in the chapter.) We carry on this exciting, unspoken language all night until the excitement builds to a point where something *has to* be done.

Eye contact means "It's ON". When I slowly turned my head to look at her, I was communicating to her that 1) I was in no rush, and 2) the dance of seduction had begun. Every time I locked eyes with her, I was topping up the tension, using my eyes to say, "We are two predators and we both know each other has what the other wants." Each time she looked at me, she was communicating her curiosity and willingness to learn more and continue the dance.

It hits midnight and I've got to get out of there. I go over to her and say, "I was wondering who was going to say something first." We then exchange a bit of conversation. Then I say, "It's unfortunate we met this way. I've got to catch the last train," and we exchange numbers.

I walk towards the stairs and get held up by a bit of conversation with someone else. She comes passing by and I just pull her in and we start making out there and then.

Now the reason I could do that so quickly is because the intensity had already built up by me positioning myself, playing on her cues, and turning up the heat throughout the night. Eye contact is the first conversation you have with someone. However, a lot of people are unaware of what to do with that language, unaware of how to start a conversation non-verbally.

Why You Should Stop Talking

Fifty-seven percent of the way we communicate comes through body language, and 35 percent from *how* we say things. The words we actually use account for a measly seven percent[1]! So we need to become aware of how we are projecting ourselves, the signals other people are giving us, and how to capitalize on opportunities.

All sorts of things can be communicated through body language: fear, jealousy, excitement, intrigue. Communicating non-verbally is exciting because it's primal, and it's discreet, which women appreciate. In our society we all want to advance towards a sexual place. However, women often are punished for it. So, we need to take that reality into consideration.

What we are looking to communicate with our body language is "I am secure in myself", which suggests to the woman "If he can handle himself, he can handle me".

Develop a ritual that puts you into that state. Whether it's listening to a certain song that gets your heart rate up or doing some activity that makes you feel like a fucking boss.

As we said in the previous chapter, effective body language comes from a place of certainty. If you're filling your head with doubt, then your body language will show as much. But if

your mindset is in a place of certainty, your body language will reflect that and so will your results.

Body Language to Look Out For

Here's the best social cues women give you to show they are intrigued:

One, they're looking at you.

If they're looking at you – and I'm happy to argue the case on this – I would say 90 per cent of the time, it's *on*. They're giving you a window to approach and talk to them. I've sat in rooms and spoke to groups of women in workshops, and we spoke quite openly about what signals they give to men.

If it's a confident, flirtatious girl, she might look over and hold that look and maybe even smile. She might even give you *the* look, and then there's no doubt about it. It's fucking *on*.

At the other end of the spectrum is the shy girl who'll look at you and then her eyes will just hit the floor. Different types of women give off different signals, but in essence, if they're looking over, you have to assume it's an opening.

And, if you go over there and it apparently wasn't, no matter. You're over there and you can work your magic!

Closing the spatial gap is another huge signal. It's no coincidence that when you last saw her, she was standing by the door and then when you next lock eyes with her, she's standing right next to you at the bar with her friends. She is giving you a window of opportunity to open her and it's up to you to pick up on that signal and capitalize on it.

You can also tell a lot from the language communicated below the waist (jokes aside). Whatever their mind is focused on, the feet will point in that direction. If her leg and body is pointed inward toward you, the interest is there. If they're outward, you need to build more rapport.

Another surefire way to tell if she's interested is physical touching. Follow the rule of three: if she touches you three times, it's *on*.

Directing the Body Language Conversation

In the same way you control the flow of a verbal conversation, you can control the flow of a body language conversation. We call this "forcing an indicator", or forcing a response.

If someone is giving you eye contact, and you just want to double confirm there's something going on there, you can do a gesture. The easiest one is just to hold up your glass and give her cheers, and if it's received well, she'll mirror that. With that, you can have 100 percent confirmation it's on.

You can play around with this idea. My friend used to do this thing where he would look at the girl and then pretend he was hiding, or pretend to do up his fly. We did a lot of things like that – little silly things that would get a response, while giving us that double confirmation.

One gambit I've done with a client is to write on a piece of paper and start playfully "texting" the girl with a piece of paper across the bar.

Another time I had a client and we spotted a girl who was a third wheel with her friend and her friend's boyfriend. She was drinking white wine, so I got the client to buy a glass of red wine, "cheers" her and swap her white wine with red.

You can also use small gestures to non-verbally communicate these things:

- **"I am secure"**: Put your hand out for her to grab.
- **"I am certain"**: Place your hand on the small of her back to direct her somewhere.
- **"I am open"**: Signal for her to come over.

Seduction Positioning

One of the most intimate things about someone is their space. If you get too close to someone, it's the equivalent of breaking into their house. You're not invited into that space, and you haven't built up enough rapport to be invited, so you need to build that rapport before you move into that level of intimacy.

In the introduction, we briefly spoke about spatial awareness. Understanding spatial awareness is one of the most overlooked aspects of seduction.

Most people fall into the trap of less spatial awareness because they haven't put the shoe on the other foot and thought, "How would I respond if someone jumped in this close to me and started speaking to me?" But there is another thing they don't ask: "In this environment, who else am I competing with in terms of getting their attention?"

If it's at night, and you're in a bar or club, the only real competition you have for her attention are the other guys, her loud friends, and the other people joining the group.

If it's in the daytime, and you're chatting with women you meet on the street, you're competing with beggars. You're competing with club promoters. You're competing with charity workers. That's a lot of undesirable people she really doesn't want to give her time away to. So, in that split-second, you've got to rise above those distractions and communicate well.

When you approach a woman, give yourself the rule of taking one step back and remaining an arm's distance away. Remember, if you're comfortable, they're comfortable. So think about the most comfortable situation you could possibly be in.

Is there a wall to lean on? If you've watched my YouTube (https://www.youtube.com/user/AboutJohnnyCassell/) videos, you'll see I'll often use a wall to lean on because I know it is the most comfortable place I could possibly be, and I'm also giving them the option to leave. Leaning against a wall also makes it look like they have stopped to hit on me.

"'Hello' is the second thing you say. Priming the interaction with your eyes is the first." – Johnny Cassell

---

Techniques:

Eye Contact Chicken

The first thing you need to be able to do is maintain eye contact. A great number of people find it awkward and uncomfortable to hold eye contact with another person, but if someone is holding eye contact with you, you can only assume they're coming from a place of certainty. When someone breaks eye contact with you, they're generally shy or insecure.

Here is an exercise you can do to get more confident with using eye contact: **start playing chicken**. When you're out and about, look to make eye contact with people and try to be the last one to break it. You can do this in shopping malls, on the street, in the club, wherever, just get used to holding eye contact more often and longer.

You have to pick your subjects wisely. But I think it's more exciting to go for people you might ordinarily find intimidating. If it's the most dangerous looking dude, and you manage to hold eye contact with them, they're likely to think, "Fuck me, this guy's crazy as fuck." (Don't get into trouble with this.)

Practise holding eye contact longer than you're used to. Go out and spend a lunchtime approaching people. Ask them where a menswear store is or whatever, and when you do, hold eye contact with them long enough to record their eye colour. That's a good enough indicator to tell you you've kept your concentration in the right place for the right amount of time.

Another thing you can do is to go out and try not to speak a word *all night*. No verbal conversations whatsoever. Then give yourself a task of communicating with a handful of people nonverbally and see how far you can take it.

Exercise: Eye Colour Bingo

Here's a fun exercise you can do to practise holding eye contact whether you're out in the daytime or at night.

1. In your journal write down five eye colours, e.g. amber, blue, brown, grey, green.
2. Hold eye contact with someone until you can mentally record their eye colour.
3. Write a brief description of the person next to the eye colour.
4. Keep going until you find one person for each colour.

Once you've completed your list, you can write it down as an achievement in your journal.

The Alexander Technique

The Alexander Technique is a posture correction technique designed by Frederick Alexander, a Shakespearean orator who initially used the technique to cure his voice loss. It goes as follows:

1. Stand with your feet shoulder-width apart.
2. Imagine a string holding up your head from the ceiling.
3. Now, imagine that string getting tighter and tighter. As the string pulls you tighter, you can feel your back arch and your ass pushing back behind you. Already you can feel your posture being corrected.
4. Finally, pull up your shoulders and just let them drop.

That is the correct posture to adopt.

Alexander realised our posture and outer presentation can affect how we feel. By developing a great posture you create a positive feedback loop, where standing properly gives you more confidence, which helps you stand more properly, and so on.

I also go to the chiropractor at least twice a month. If you've experienced any back pain or have recurring back pain, I reccommend getting some advice from these guys.

Here's a piece from my Chiropractor, Dr Andrew Garbett DC MChiro BSc, (check out his website, http://www.andygarbett.com):

'Stand up straight, stop slouching!' I'm sure you've heard these words a few (hundred) times as a kid. Like most repetitive phrases passed down through generations there's some good reasoning for why we should pay attention to our posture, as a kid as well as an adult.

As a child, those words are aimed at aesthetics, the way we look, slouching or being hunched over is seen as less appealing to the eye than a nice, strong, upright posture. Parents wouldn't want everyone seeing their kids in a posture that suggests insecurity and lack of strength, as it can be perceived as a reflection on them.

Now 'good' posture from a purely anatomical point of view can be described as the composition of the positioning of all body segments at a given point in time. This means where your body parts are, your head, shoulders, hips, feet, at certain times, when standing, sitting, even moving, will determine whether you have good posture or not.

Good posture will have small variances with each individual but follows the basic principles, so when standing you should try and stand as tall as possible with your head high but face pointing forward. Shoulder blades pulled back and

chest high, brace your stomach and keep your feet pointing forward

This is the ultimate goal but anywhere close will put your body in a better position than what it previously was. This position shouts out confidence, someone who is comfortable with themselves.

It gives others a sense of curiosity towards you – 'they look like they have something about them, wonder what their story is?'.

Your posture and body language can be that powerful.

If we don't concentrate on our posture, our body tissue changes and our body parts move into less desired positions. As you continue to stay in an awkward posture, the likelihood of your body putting them back where they should be becomes less likely.

As we stand and move it does not 'undo' the changes, the body simply finds another way to move. For example, say we have now developed a "rounded shoulders head forward" position from years of sitting at a desk. When we change positions from sitting to standing, instead of our body bringing the shoulder blades back and down and bringing the head back over our body, lining up our ears with the middle of our shoulders, it simply makes smaller movements.

It's less effort for the body to do this but because of the positions it has been in for many years, certain areas that we should move from are now stiff and simply unable to move like they should. You can see how this process can go unnoticed for years and years and happen all over the body, not just the shoulders and neck.

Practising good posture can reduce these changes or stop this process from developing to a point where it's hard to undo

and prevents leading to more serious issues occurring in the future.

As well as the physical, structural changes that occur with having bad posture there are internal changes that occur too. Research carried out at Harvard Business School has shown that hormonal changes occur when we put our body into an upright, open, powerful position.

A position of confidence and presence allowed testosterone levels (the 'dominance hormone') to increase to nearly 20 per cent compared to baseline levels of participants prior to the experiment and a 25 per cent decrease in the stress hormone cortisol.

The researchers also found the opposite to be true.

By sitting or standing in a closed position with arms crossed across chest, legs crossed, slouching, making yourself smaller, the effects on hormones were also noticed; after spending just two minutes in these postures testosterone levels decreased by around 15 per cent and cortisol levels increased by 10 per cent. So not only will you look less confident and shy, but you will feel that way too.

Based on this research it begs the question 'can you fake it until you make it?'. If you put yourself into a dominant posture for two minutes or more on a regular basis, will this change your habits? The answer is "yes". Not only will it change your habit of adopting better posture so that other people's perceptions of you are different, more positive, but it will actually change who you become and the way you feel.

If practised for long enough there will be a point where you won't even notice you are doing it and almost forgetting what you were once like.

The easiest way to come across as a confident, strong, dominant person, is simply to be one.

Common Body Language Mistakes (and How to Fix Them)

Throughout my time helping clients improve their seduction technique, I have repeatedly seen different students making the same mistakes. These are the most common errors:

Holding your drink in front of your body

Whether you have your drink covering your stomach or chest, this is *closed* body language, and it's a reflection of how you're feeling inside. Whether you intend it to or not, it's communicating "Don't talk to me", and it prevents people from entering your space.

When I catch my students doing this, I grab their finger and just move it to the side, so it opens up that gate. My students are normally never aware of this when I first do it to them, but if you get in the habit of just having your drink to your side, you will instantly look 10 times more approachable.

Standing with your feet close together

If you're in a busy environment, there's nothing worse than someone walking past you and you rocking back and forth or looking like you're falling over. It looks pathetic and weak. When your feet are too close together, you don't have strong grounding and can't take the bump.

Leaning in

Leaning in is another bad body language habit. Whether your neck is leaning in or the whole upper half of your body is leaning forward, when you do this, you're invading her space and you're not making use of your size. It looks needy and it

suggests you're uncomfortable. If you've got height, use it to your advantage. Don't compensate your height for someone else.

If you can't hear someone, just stand there, and say, "I can't hear you. Come closer." Or sit down. Use it as a reason to go find a place to sit down together so you can keep talking.

Hands in pockets

You're not at school. If your hands are glued to your pockets, you're missing out on a great opportunity to "escalate". Escalation is where you turn up the heat in a conversation through physical touching or taking the conversation to a more sexual place.

A lot of subtle escalation building techniques I use come from me just talking and expressing myself. But I also may subtly reach out and touch them on the shoulder, on the leg, on the back, or I may even move them around, but I can't do any of this if my hands are glued to my pockets.

Moving quickly

The general rule for having great body language is *slow everything down*. Think about all the Bond films you've ever seen. Look how calm, cool, and collected James Bond is. Even when he wins a game of poker in *Casino Royale*, do you see him leave the table and rush to the cashier to cash in his chips? No. You see him leave the table calm, cool and collected, and glide through the casino like a piece of silk.

If you want to be attractive, you need to look as if you are in control of every move you make. This means becoming conscious of your movements. When you pick up your glass, do you grab it or do you slowly pick up your glass from the bar? When you go to touch your hair, are you scratching your hair nervousy or adjusting it to make it more seductive? When you're walking, are you rushing around or are you slowly gliding through? Build more intention into your movements, and practise them slowly.

Spatial Positioning

First things first, very rarely is it safe to approach a woman on her own at the bar. She's either waiting for a date to turn up, or waiting for a friend who has just come out of the loo.

If there's two of them, or if it's a group, it's a lot better. I'm going to run through a few examples of how to position yourself when you're approaching groups of two or more at a bar.

First of all, you need to make sure everyone gets eye contact. If you don't address everyone with your eyes, then you run the risk of someone not feeling included, and they could be the reason why the interaction fails.

If someone is being a bit quiet or distant, just stop what you're doing and bring them in, saying something like, "I didn't catch your name". Just pull them in and make sure everyone is included.

Approaching a group at a table

If you see a group of women sitting at a table, the most sophisticated approach is nonverbal, via eye contact. Just select one of the women at the table, then pull over a waiter, so you can subtly find out and order another round of whatever they are drinking.

Don't go over right away. Rather, use that round of drinks as a token of mystery, leaving them feeling curious as to why

you've sent one over and haven't come over yourself. Nine times out of ten, they'll come over to you and thank you at some point or maybe towards the end of the night. That one person out of ten who doesn't come isn't really worth knowing anyway.

Another approach, if you've had a bit of eye contact going on throughout the night, is to go over there and ask everyone's permission to isolate a friend. You can say, "Girls, I wanted to ask your permission first before I went ahead and just did this. Would you mind if I borrow your friend for a second?" After their friends say, "Oh no, sure, go ahead", it's very likely the friend is going to be more compliant to go with you to the bar.

Another one is to go over and make eye contact with someone and just say, "Oh my god, how have you been?" Have her feel a bit confused and then say, "Oh my god, I'm coming in. Budge up." Then go over and sit next to her and just play along with the bullshit like you know her from somewhere. Her friends aren't going to know any different.

Dance floor approach

This is a big trouble area for men. The biggest mistake men make on the dance floor is they approach the dance floor and try to get that cheap grind going on, which they probably will get, but that's probably all they'll get.

Unless you are extremely talented in that department, I would only use the dance floor as a place of humour. Go with your friend and take the piss out of each other mirroring dance moves and have some fun. Women will find the two of you attractive because you look like two guys having fun rather than two guys trying to vulture some woman off the dance floor. That gives you a platform to then transition to taking the piss out of their dance moves. It can also give you a platform to isolate them off the dance floor.

Don't go in for that cheap grind. You will get it, but they'll only experience buyer's remorse because they got too intimate too fast.

Takeaways

Your body language and spatial positioning communicate a lot about you. With poor positioning and posture, you can turn people off before you even open your mouth. Work on projecting confidence and comfort.

1. **If there's eye contact, it's on:** Eye contact is your signal that someone is interested in you. If you see someone eyeballing you, you've got to talk to them.
2. **Slow down:** Be mindful of every movement you make, and *slow* it down. Sexy equals condfidence equals certainty, and people with certainty can take their time.
3. **Ground yourself:** Put yourself in the moment. Your outer body presents your inner self; if you're nervous or uncomfortable on the inside, you're going to need to work extra hard to hide it.
4. **Re-read this chapter:** There are a lot of techniques and information in this chapter. Re-read it to make sure you've absorbed all the lessons.

Chapter Four: Case Study

Name: Ben
Age: 24
Profession: PR

What areas of your dating world did Johnny work with you on?

We worked on approaching beautiful women

How did working with Johnny on Body Language and Spatial Awareness change your life?

Working with Johnny and his laid back approaches, such as holding a coffee and putting an arm on the wall, helped me approach a number of ladies I would not have dreamed of before.

Which of the techniques that Johnny taught you do you still use on a regular basis?

Easier to have a conversation with a woman at the bar than around the venue, as it's an easy exit for both parties if the conversation becomes stilted.

How did working with Johnny help you outside of the dating world?

It helped me appreciate that it is possible to open a conversation with a stranger that you may wish to speak to and develop as a contact for future business opportunities.

What was the most valuable lesson Johnny taught you?

Not to put women on a pedestal and with all interactions I offer 50% of the value.

For more resources and access to **'5 Seduction Secrets High-Class Women WISH you knew'**, head over to *www.JohnnyCassell.com/BookResources*

CHAPTER FIVE:
Competent Conversation

"When you are predictable you are too familiar"
– Johnny Cassell

By far the two biggest questions I get are, "What should I say?" and, "What should my opening line be?". Here's the crazy thing.

It *doesn't* matter.

A lot of people spend a lot of time thinking about the correct opening line or the best ice breaker, when actually, it doesn't really matter what you say. It's what you say *in response* to their response.

With all the tips and techniques you pick up throughout this book, ultimately what you're trying to do is get an initial response from them, so it gives you something to play with.

In this chapter, you're going to learn a lot about conversation structure, the flow of it, and what direction to take it. One of the key mechanisms you're going to learn about is the "hook". The hook is a conversational topic that allows you to move further along the conversation structure. A lot of guys struggle with this because they don't actually *listen* to women's responses.

Once you've mastered the ability of conversation, you've moved a step closer to being able to build relationships with *whomever* you choose. I've said it before. If you become great at building relationships, there's nothing you can't do. *Everything* is built on relationships.

These conversational tools are not just for finding the woman of your dreams. You can (and should) use these tools in your workplace, with your family, and in your everyday interactions. You can use them to create the life you want.

Story: A Gentleman's Lourve-ly Liaison

So, I'd just broken up with my long-term girlfriend. Needless to say I was on a bit of an emotional rollercoaster. I kept myself busy with work, but I still had the wind knocked out of my sails.

I was out with a client, and we were in this swanky bar in Mayfair. I was still sharp with my conversational ability, but I knew that logically I should be operating at a higher level. I just wasn't emotionally *there*. So, my student was speaking to these girls, and one of the girls asks, "What do you do?"

I feel a sudden surge of endorphins, like something inside me has suddenly switched on. I start smiling inside, and I say, "I'm a plastic surgeon."

"Plastic surgeon?" she asks.

"Mmm," I say, "I've pretty much seen every size, colour, and shape of a woman's breasts." She's captivated, so I add, "Apart from yours."

In that moment, it was like my team had just scored a goal. It didn't matter about her response. I was *back*. I was on the road to recovery!

Inspired by that one event, I put together a workshop in Paris with my friend Garrett, and we took a couple of guys out to the Louvre to practise daytime approaches.

Walking around, I see this "Russian Bond Girl" with knee-high leather boots, orange tan pencil skirt and white blouse with a few buttons undone to reveal the cups at the top of her breasts. I'm dressed like the classic English gent with beige pants, some brown loafers, and a well-fitted Barbour jacket; I couldn't look more British if I tried.

I stroll over to her. "Excuse me, you know where the Mona Lisa is?"

"No, I'm looking for it," she says.

"You're lost too?" I ask and hold eye contact with her. "Well I can only suggest we find it together."

We go off to find this painting and it becomes this magical experience. Every step we took was so smooth, it all led up to the moment of reaching the painting. Each footstep we took built up the anticipation. Remember when I said that it's up to you to create the fairy tale? Well, standing there, looking at that painting, it was one of those moments – a "Wow" moment. Then we go on to walk further and I just stop.

I decide to take a risk.

I slowly move my head towards her eye line, and she looks back at me.

"I have to be honest," I say.

"What?" she asks.

"All I've been thinking about for the last 15 minutes is slowly unbuttoning your blouse button by button, peeling out your breasts and circling my tongue around your nipples."

She gives me this look like a laser beam as if she were saying "are you fucking serious?" to see if I am being for real or not, but I just hold my ground and give her a look that says "yes, I fucking am". Blood rushes to her cheeks and I can tell she's turned on by my boldness.

I break the moment and say "shall we?" and we walk on. Each step builds the anticipation toward something that neither of us can quite put our finger on, but *something* is going to happen between us.

We sit down in an alcove and I start unloading my thoughts about what I was going to do to her in her left ear. As I feel her getting hotter in the moment, I get up and lead her to the Terrasse de Pomone, overlooking the Louvre.

Now I don't like women that smoke, but in this moment, in this *scene*, in this movie we were creating between us she had to. I ordered tea for both of us and played up to the "English gentleman" stereotype that I'd created.

I spotted the rest of the group I was leading and counted how many steps it was going to take for them to reach the table. I timed the interaction perfectly so that the team I was with could watch as I pulled in this woman whom I'd met 20 minutes ago and made out with her in full daylight.

When you take a risk like that, women will look at you to see if you are being sincere. Because I was coming from that place of certainty, she realized, *Holy shit, this guy is for real.* Unfortunately, she turned out to be married and I have a moral code, so that was the end of that.

Did you see how boring the conversation topic was? I literally asked her for directions and then it turned into a story she probably still thinks about in private moments. So stop worrying about what to say. Just fucking say *something* and play off people's responses.

With that said, let's look at some ways you can reliably get people to open up.

"People always start conversations with what they are missing" – Johnny Cassell

---

Everyone's Favourite Subject...

Everyone's favourite subject is themselves. It makes sense. It's nice to feel validated, and we don't get a chance to talk about ourselves often. We don't get to tell people our dreams or our stories. So when someone comes along and just listens, that's a very powerful moment.

When most guys talk to women, they only talk about themselves. What they end up doing is leaving very little for the woman to find out. If you're talking too much, you're not playing the man of mystery, and if she knows every corner of your life instantly, why does she need to see you again?

It's rare to find someone you can share the intimate parts of your life with, but this is a desire everyone has. So when you ask the right questions and use the right language, you can get to some "forbidden" places, and that is when you become a good conversationalist.

Why Your Ears Make Women Want You

Another reason why I'm shocked at how many people ask "What should I say?" is because when you're *talking* to women, you shouldn't be saying much of anything. Instead you need to listen. If you don't listen, you're not going to get to know *her* nor be able to build that rapport.

Listening is sexy because you're not giving much away. You're actually taking control of the conversation. You have more power than the other person because you can "see their cards". And by listening, you generate intrigue. You're now a challenge. You're different.

Through listening you're breaking a very annoying pattern. When most men go out, they talk about themselves, trying to impress women by telling them what job they have or what car they drive. You know, generic boring shit. These guys (your competition) don't give women the opportunity to tell *their* story.

By asking sincere questions and listening, you're actually breaking a behavioural pattern expected in that environment.

When you listen you're still communicating with the other person, but you're now communicating that you're interested and that they are important. You're also communicating that you're not insecure about yourself because you're not trying so hard to seek approval.

The Power of the Challenge

When you do speak, it's important to offer a "challenge". All this means is that you challenge their response rather than just take it as a given. When you challenge someone, you will actually see their eyes go up diagonally. That means they're trying to access their thought catalogue, which means they're invested. And if they're invested in the conversation, it means they're invested in you.

For more information about how to tell what people are thinking, head over to www.JohnnyCassell.com/bookresources.

Here's an example. If I talk to someone and their accent is not from the UK, I may say, "Where is your accent from?" That's my assumption. I'm assuming they're from somewhere else. Let's pretend they say Brazil. I then respond, "Brazil? I've never been to Brazil. If I was to spend a long weekend there, how would you recommend I spend it? Give me three places to check out."

That's a much better response than if they say "Brazil" and you respond "Cool. What do you do?". That communicates to them, "I'm not really listening. I don't give a shit. I'm just thinking about how quickly I can get you into bed."

By challenging them, you're breaking a pattern because you're listening and making them think about their response. Then you can move the conversation deeper below the surface.

Challenging builds attraction because it shows them you're conversationally gifted. When guys go out, they normally don't challenge women. They're a bobble head, sitting on a car's dashboard, bobbing their head in agreement with everything the woman says – not really listening.

It's even okay to challenge in a way that promotes conflict. I'm not saying you should go out picking fights, but let me just say that it's far more attractive to create conflict than to remain neutral. Conflict gives you a chance to get to know them, and it gives them a chance to see you stand your ground.

Is She qualified?

Earlier on in the book we discussed making a visual list of things you find attractive, including character traits. We also talked about long-term investment: no matter if you're looking to get laid or have a long-term relationship, you *need* to be spending time with high-quality women.

That brings us to "qualifying".

Qualification is when you screen someone by setting up criteria for them to meet before they can be approved. Women do this all the time but for some reason we don't do this to women.

Most men don't know how to qualify a woman because they base a woman's value on her looks and look past any negative traits she may possess. They haven't spent time thinking about what it is they truly want from a partner; therefore, they settle for for someone who doesn't fit their criteria.

Once you get a good conversation going, the next step is qualifying the woman based on her character. That means returning to your list of ideal traits. For example, if one of your requirements is that you want her to be health and fitness orientated, some language you could use would be, "For me, I love a woman that looks after herself. What do you do to maintain yourself in such a way?"

She might say she doesn't go to the gym – that she's just gifted naturally. Or she might say, "I play squash once a week. I cycle to work. I go running." When she effectively jumps through your hoop, she is seeking approval, and you should most certainly grant her the validation she deserves because she is meeting your requirement. If, however, there is someone who doesn't meet your requirement by demonstrating a trait you're not too fond of, you need to learn how to disqualify them.

For example, I may not like a girl who smokes. It doesn't mean I wouldn't date a girl who smokes. I just need to make sure she knows I don't like it, not by fathering her or telling her off, just by demonstrating my disiniterest. When she goes to draw out a cigarette, I might say, "Oh, you smoke," letting her realize smoking is not something that's in line with my values. I'm not directly telling her, "Don't smoke," but she gets it. Then, you can reward her if she corrects her behaviour.

Always leave people better than when you found them. Say you're talking to a woman who fits all your physical criteria but makes a racist joke. Don't father her, but let her know racism isn't in line with your values.

If the character trait so offends your values that you don't want to spend any time with her, break rapport. If I'm in a bar and I lose interest in a subject, I will just start looking at my phone, or I may swivel outwards on my bar stool and stop looking at them. Then, I may not give her attention when she tries to correct herself or apologises for her behaviour.

You need to qualify every single person, not just women, in your life. If you're going to invest your emotional energy and time into a woman, a friend or an associate, you owe it to them and yourself to make sure they are a good fit.

"Reverse engineer the conversation." – Johnny Cassell

Techniques:

Basic Conversation Structure

What I'm going to show you is a basic conversational template you can use for *any* situation. I'll go through what each of the terms mean and offer examples and exercises you can use to create your own conversations.

The basic conversation structure is:

1. Open
2. Assumption
3. Hook
4. Challenge/Relate
5. Time Constraint
6. Close

NOTE: qualification and escalation exist outside of the conversational model. This model is designed primarily to create a positive impact. Qualification and escalation are switches to turn up the heat and get her to communicate interest to you or have her try to seduce you.

Open

The opening line is the least important part of the structure. It's so unimportant that I don't even use it. I normally just jump straight in with a challenge. That being said, I would advise you guys to start here.

Most great openers are assumption-based; here are some classics:

- I can't work out where that accent is from.
- Where did you get that tan?
- Your mum's Italian, right?
- How long have you two been sisters?
- Which one's the birthday girl?
- What are you girls celebrating?
- You're such an only child.

If you want, come up with your own assumptions. Look at your list of character traits of your ideal woman and base your assumptions on things that qualify them. For example, if one of the traits you're looking for is "nerdy", you could open with something like, "I bet you're a huge Harry Potter nerd."

All we're doing with the opener is looking for a conversational hook. Earlier, we used the assumption that the woman wasn't from the UK, so we said, "Where's that accent from?" and she said, "I'm from Brazil." So the hook is Brazil.

Hooks

Hooks are conversational topics, and they can be divided into two categories: "low-calibre" and "high-calibre". Low-calibre hooks are things like: someone's job, the weather, traffic conditions, their favourite colour. High-calibre hooks are much jucier.

In our Brazil example, we were talking about language. That is a high-calibre hook because there's a lot of conversation that can come from language. It's attached to travel, culture, and traditions. It's a fantastic hook to use and it's always my go-to method when available.

Here's a list of high-calibre hooks you can use to build assumptions:

- Celebrities/entertainers
- Arts
- Movies
- Music
- Theatre
- Exercise/Sports
- History
- Current affairs
- Pop culture
- Travel
- Culture
- Experiences
- Emotions
- Family
- Countries

I would suggest you only go for hooks you can personally relate to for two reasons. The first is you need to be able to have some conversational content of your own to contribute. If you're talking about Yoga, but don't have any idea what you're talking about, it puts you in a weaker position because you're clearly pandering to the woman's interests. The second reason is *you* should be entertained by these conversations. If you don't give a shit about celebrities, you don't want to spend 10 minutes listening to someone talking about why Justin Bieber might be going out with Scarlet Johansson.

Challenge/Relate

Once you've got the conversational hook, you need to challenge. As we discussed earlier, this means diving deeper into the topic and exploring what they have to say.

Coming back to our Brazil example, maybe I haven't ever been to Brazil, so I can ask, "What are the three places I should definitely check out if I spend a long weekend there?"

When she responds, you can challenge further by saying, "Don't tell me the touristy places. I want to know about the real places – where the locals go" or, "Tell me something quite scandalous about Brazil". Look for something you need to say to challenge them, so you can accumulate unique content. Then, if you ever meet a Brazilian again, you will have something more niche to say to them.

Look beyond the conversation you're having at the time and think about the bigger picture. Look to gain knowledge and become worldly and wise from all the people you meet. It's only going to strengthen your relationships.

Once you have that insider knowledge, you can "Relate" to stories instead of challenging them. When you relate, you're diving into the bank of knowledge you already have on the subject. You don't need to challenge because you have content on the subject.

For example, once I've found out that she's from Brazil, I might talk about a friend who moved there, became an English teacher, and has started *capoeira*. From there, I can talk about how I studied *capoeira* myself.

When you feel you can relate to the conversation topic, that's when you should contribute. If she asks you about your life, then share.

By sharing my story of how I studied *capoeira*, I communicate that I'm an open-minded, cultured man. I'm communicating things we might have in common (in this case "dance" and learning about different cultures). Ultimately, I'm communicating this: "I'm familiar with your world".

The idea of finding someone similar to you has been hammered into our brains since we were young. There's an innate prejudice against people outside of our culture, background, or class that says "you don't understand me". By relating through stories and knowledge. we demonstrate a connection that goes deeper than shallow stereotypes.

Time constraints

Most guys think if you meet a charming lady, you should make yourself as available as possible.

Bullshit.

Human beings value scarcity. The more scarce you are, the more valuable you seem.

That brings me to "time-constraints". Here are a few:

- "You know what? I've really got to run off because I'm supposed to meet my friend at twelve."
- "You know what? I got to get out of here. I shouldn't even be speaking to you right now. I could get into trouble. I'm already late as it is."
- "Listen, I've got to get out of here because at midnight my taxi turns back into a pumpkin."

Then you can naturally lead that into a conversation about continuing the conversation.

When you feel like the conversation is getting exciting, you need to cut it off at a high. We want them to associate us with being fun and exciting, so avoid ending the conversation in a dry patch, also known as the "yawn zone".

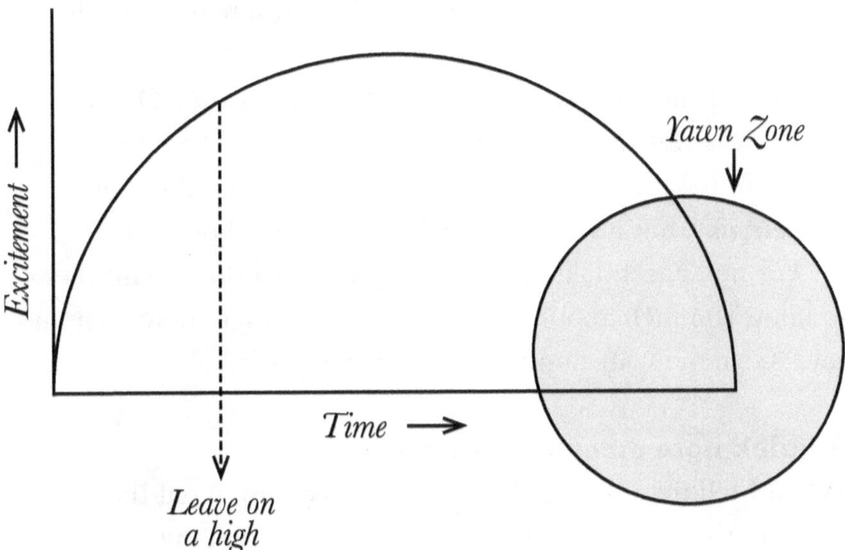

The yawn zone comes when the conversation has surpassed the initial period of excitement and you're trying to extend it because you've met a great woman who seems to have something in common with you. In actual fact, you're completely milking the udders of the interaction until there's nothing left in the tank.

Instead, give them a reason to want to see you again. It's a very difficult habit to get into, but ending a conversation at the moment of greatest excitement is the perfect formula to leave them wanting more. Imagine your favourite TV shows. They end at the peak of intrigue – at a cliffhanger. You want to do the same thing with your conversations.

That brings us to the "close".

Close

The next chapter is *all* about the close, so we'll quickly define the process here. "Closing" is about getting the number, having a quick kiss, or even having sex (I'll show you how to do all three in the next chapter).

One of the most effective ways of closing is the "Open question" close. This is where you say, "What's the best way to stay in touch?" Now, they may say "phone number" or "Facebook", but it's up to you which one you choose.

For me, Facebook is fine. But sometimes I don't want them to know so much about me so quickly, so I might play on it and say, "Give me your number. We're not 16 here."

A quick note on compliments

When I tell my intermediate students to compliment the woman, they're often initially surprised because, out in the bars or coffee shops, you typically don't want to lead with a compliment about a woman's body. This is because, A: she's heard it a million times before, and B: there's no emotional weight to the compliment. At that point, you're just some guy.

However, everyone loves a compliment from someone they care about. So when there comes a time when you want to escalate the situation, go ahead and give her a sincere and specific compliment.

Imagine you're driving a car. There's only so long you can go around driving in first gear. So think of the compliment as a gear shift. By giving her a compliment, you're climbing the hill of escalation.

But you have to have that escalation in your mind. You have to flick that switch. If you don't, you're not going to turn her on. If you take her back to the hotel or to your apartment, or whatever, and you're not showing your intent, then she's just going to think you're gay or just a "nice guy".

The Power of Admitting Ignorance

One of my golden rules is: "Whatever you find yourself ignorant towards is something you need to learn more about".

If you go through life with an "I know everything" attitude, you're cutting yourself off from some amazing experiences. Similarly, you can't base an opinion on something you know nothing about. Rather than staying fenced in with your mouth shut about a subject, or having an opinion based on nonsense, you need to go exploring.

If you're meeting a certain type of person from a certain country, why not go visit the country and explore the culture so you can understand it. Likewise, if people are talking about a certain subject that's quite big in the media, and you know nothing about it, you should go learn what you can. Seduction can be a by-product of the larger goal of exploring your curiosity.

By taking an active interest in the world around you, you build your strength in conversation and put yourself above the 80 percent of people who just say silly things or say nothing at all. Also, by attending seminars or workshops, it allows you to meet new circles of people you would never normally even think about meeting, so don't limit yourself.

Same with language. It's ignorant when you're travelling somewhere to expect everyone to speak English. I was that way for a very long time, but now I find great joy and confidence in learning a little bit of the language from all the places I go. When you do that, you instantly gain a lot of respect from the locals you meet.

Knowledge gives you an edge. By admitting your ignorance and being open to learning new things, you can have amazing conversations with so many different types of people.

Building Your Conversational Bank

Listening, challenging, relating, and learning are all ways to gather new content, and acquiring new conversational content immediately puts you ahead of your competition. If you take the "I know nothing, but I'm intrigued" approach to life, you can build relationships on a global scale.

There are no limits.

Think of it as a challenge. When I first came to London, I didn't know anything about Russian girls, and I realized, if I wanted to be able to connect with this sort of girl, I'd have to accumulate content showing I'm not just an ignorant English guy expecting them to connect with me on that level.

So I "challenged" these girls on things about their culture, their way of life and their history, and I accumulated a ton of content I was then able to use in my conversations moving forward with other Russian women.

I learned about the government blinding the architect behind the Saint Basil's cathedral, and I came up with a theory on why Russian people are so closed – because they feel the government has lied to them for so many years.

When I expressed these facts and opinions, the Russian women I met were surprised and respected me for having that knowledge. I would say, for a few of them, I was actually teaching them a thing or two about their own culture.

Your looks will only get you so far. Your looks will get you a foot in the door, but they do not define your success with women. If you show you have substance beyond visual attraction, then you're moving close to having that second foot into the bedroom.

If you want to know what a great conversation is, you first need to understand what a shit conversation is. A shit conversation is the same kind of conversation you repeatedly have with new people, e.g. "What do you do?" "Where are you from?" and "How old are you?". If you want to make an impact you have to break that pattern.

A great conversation is one that moves in the direction of stimulation, and there's a simple way to tell if a conversation is stimulating: It keeps you interested. I find a conversation stimulating when:

- I have to think about my response.
- My ideas are challenged.
- Someone introduces a sexual element to the conversation.
- Someone introduces a topic I'm familiar with and have an appreciation for.

All of these conversational elements are stimualting because they move beyond the surface. If you want to break the pattern and deeply connect, you need to use these concepts in your conversation.

Takeaways

The most important aspect of conversation is that you *start* them. Even a mundane conversation that begins with "Hello" can be seductive. However, once you learn how to stimulate people's minds with challenging and relating, you're well on your way to becoming a master of seduction.

1. **People love to talk about themselves**: The easiest way to get people to open up is to ask them a question about who they are and what they think.

2. **Listen:** When you listen more than you speak, it communicates that you're confident, gives you an air of mystery, and makes the other person feel special.

3. **Qualify everyone**: You need to make sure the people around you are truly amazing and match your values. Don't let yourself become surrounded by those at odds with who you are.

4. **Leave them better than you found them:** Seek to give everyone you meet a positive experience, and once they've hit the peak, leave. They'll then come and find you, or you can easily start a conversation with them again.

5. **Be curious**: Your mindset shouldn't be "get laid". Your mindset needs to be "meet interesting people". Take a genuine interest in those around you, and learn who they are. You'll end up learning so much about the world and about yourself.

Chapter Five: Case Study

Name: Keri
Age: 30
Profession: Electrical Consultant

What areas of your dating world did Johnny work with you on?

Starting from the basics, we first went out and started chatting to girls. Really starting from the ground up.

How did working with Johnny on Conversational ability change your life?

I used to be huge, so before I met Johnny I had to lose a lot of weight. I did 9 months of training and lost 10 stone.

Now, I want to go out and talk to women and Johnny's helped me raise my interactional ability and helped move my life forward.

Which of the techniques that Johnny taught you do you still use on a regular basis?

Eye contact. Before I didn't have any eye contact with anyone. Johnny told me to turn it into a game and now when I'm walking along I can look people in the eye and that's helped a huge amount.

Now that I've got confidence with that it's helped a lot because I've realised that everyone else is uncomfortable with themselves and I've realised the importance of confidence making you stand out.

How did working with Johnny help you outside of the dating world?

Before, at work, I'd just sit in the corner and do what I need to do. My interaction with colleagues was minimal. Now

*that I've got a lot more confidence and can look people in
the eye, my directors have started talking to me more.*

*So, Johnny's techniques have helped me professionally
as I've evolved how I can interact with people.*

What was the most valuable lesson Johnny taught you?
*Don't give a shit. You either win or you learn. If you have a
negative interaction, who cares? We're all born and we all die,
you can't spend your life worrying about what others think
about you. Just learn from your mistakes and move on.*

For access to more exclusive techniques and the **'5 Seduction
Secrets High-Class Women Wish You Knew'**,
www.JohnnyCassell.com/BookResources

CHAPTER SIX:
Closing

"If you're uncertain, she's uncertain" - Johnny Cassell

A lot of guys trip up on closing and it makes no sense. After employing the tools from the previous chapter and getting good at building your conversation skills, you should now have the ability to make a massive impact on people's lives.

So why don't you ask for that number?

Think about being on the receiving end of all this. People don't normally have great conversations. They get caught up with small talk. And then here you are. You've come out of nowhere, talked to them and lifted them up. You added value and made them feel great about themselves, and then you *don't* offer a way to stay in contact?!

When we meet someone we have something in common with, we need to keep them close to us. Honestly, it's weirder you *not* going for the number than you going for it. I've lost count of how many times I've been watching students have fantastic interactions with women. Then they come back over to me, and I say, "How did it go?"

"It went really well," they say. "We really connected."
"Great, you got the number, right?"

"Oh, no, I didn't get the number."

Nine times out of ten, I'll send them back in there, and nine times out of ten, they'll always get the number.

Our automatic response is to say "No" to things like this. We say "No" because it keep us in our comfort zone, but a lot of the time our comfort zone is not where we want to be. Think of it this way. If you ask for their number, you are at least giving *them* another opportunity to meet you again, so even if you go for the number and she says no, you've at least allowed her to think, "Oh wow, shit, that really happened".

People find it hard to close because they're not really in the habit of doing it. It's a weird experience for them. My students have conversations with a complete random stranger on the street, or a coffee shop, or whatever environment, and it's usually a completely new practice for them.

The trick is to get in the habit of going for the close.

I've gone out with clients, and when they were speaking to their women, I would just be having a conversation with the women next to me to keep them occupied, and I would get their numbers anyway. I wasn't necessarily interested in them, nor even attracted to them. But I want to stay in the habit of always going through the process. When someone does catch my eye, I don't have to worry about that fear of rejection because I've already programmed my mind to operate in that way.

This is about mastering a habit, and this is something we can all do. None of us has to think about how to tie up our shoelaces, but at one point in our life, we had to learn every single step. And that's exactly what I want you guys to do. I want you to go through every step; otherwise, you're just wasting your time.

Remember, it's weirder to *not* go for the number. Think about how she sees it. She knows you're hitting on her. Let me repeat that: she *knows* you're hitting on her. But when you don't go for the number, she's left thinking, "What the fuck was that all about?" She's checking her pockets, her bag, thinking you may be a pickpocket. At least out of pure decency give her the reassurance you were actually trying to pick her up.

By the end of this chapter, I'm going to give you a handful of tried and tested techniques, along with the correct language on how to solicit a number from a woman you just met, how to solicit a date right then and there, and if you feel a bit gutsy, how to move to sex on the same day.

Story: The Chances of This Happening Again? Two in a Brazilian

I recently had a client named Fernando, a fantastic French-Moroccan guy, very enthusiastic about self-development and fluent in several languages. But when he came over here, he didn't know how to dress, and he didn't know how to present himself. He also hadn't dated for a very long time, and with him coming to London, everything was new. He had to learn how to interact with the culture. But his sole goal was to get better with women.

One lovely, hot summer afternoon, Fernando and I were out doing a session together. I spotted two girls who looked like they were from out of town. They had big sunglasses on, hair down to their shoulders, and were wearing short shorts and sandals.

Now, if you're a tourist and you're travelling, you're in a certain mindset. You want to see as much as you can see and

taste all the flavours. If it's a bit of holiday romance, you'll take it, and you'll allow yourself to do a lot more because it's safe and non-judgemental.

I have this in mind and I tell him, "I want you to approach those two girls and take them on an instant date." He agrees and I keep an eye on him.

He approaches them, chats them up, then bounces them over to Green Park, where they end up getting a coffee. They then go for a walk, and I begin texting him with instructions since this is all new to him.

But from where I'm sitting, I can tell, it's going well. They're from out of town. They look Brazilian and they're probably liberated in that South American way. So I text him, "It's *on*, see it as it's *on* with *both of them*."

So Fernando starts taking care of both of them, escalating with both of them. And then I suggest that he go and do some touristy things with them, so I say, "Go and see the London Eye."

He does and I start thinking about the logistics of it all. As they're leaving the Eye, I say, "You've got it! Now use a transition to put them closer to where you live. Mention that you're hungry and you want to cook for them." So he does and then moves them from Central London to where he lives in Camden – a good 15 or 20 minutes in the cab.

Once there, he goes to a shop to get all the groceries then walks these girls into his apartment, all the while maintaining a flirtation with both of them and keeping the vibe going.

When they get inside, he puts the groceries in the kitchen, then goes to one of the girls and says, "I want to show you my weight room."

He takes her upstairs and shows her his exercise equipment. Then he starts making out with her and they start having sex.

Her friend then comes upstairs. She sits there and just starts watching for a bit. Then he says, "It's okay. Come, join in." Then they just start having this three-way. These are the same two girls he met no more than two hours before on the street.

Now Fernando was able to move things in that direction very quickly because of a number of factors. One, the girls felt safe, and they knew they weren't going to be judged. Two, this was something they obviously wanted to experience. It didn't necessarily have to come home with them. And three, they enjoyed being led into the seduction.

If we unpack that, break it down, it really comes down to expectation. In your head, you have to start from where you want things to end. If the destination is your apartment, you should be thinking, "Okay, I need to build rapport. I need to build comfort with them. I need to plant seeds and be suggestive." Then lead them to that place and put the right transitions in place for it to happen.

Story: A High Calibre Number in a Flash

When I was 18, I was going out and experimenting with all these different techniques. At the time, there was this big trend of using magic tricks. I wasn't too big into that, but out of curiosity, I bought some flash paper.

Flash paper is this paper you can light, and it just goes up super quick – like 10 times faster than normal paper would burn. When you do it, it looks like you've got a pyrotechnic in your pocket.

I was at a club called *Liquid* in Windsor. I don't know if it still exists but it's one of those commercial places where everyone goes because they've got nowhere better to go.

I see this girl and she is *high calibre* – her beauty was something I didn't have reference of. Tall, skinny, model-esque features, someone who at the time I didn't believe I could acquire. I get chatting to her and I say, "You got to believe me now, I've got a photographic memory."

"All right," she says.

"I tell you what," I say. "We're going to do a test. Give me a bit of paper, and write your number on it."

She writes her number and I say, "I'll look at this for a second," before I look at it and roll it up in my hand. "You know what we're going to do?" I ask. "I'm going to light this up right in front of you, right now. I'm going to burn it. If I remember your number, I'll call you and we'll have a drink."

"Okay," she says with excitement in her eyes.

I take the paper, walk over to the nearest guy I can find, switch the paper with a flash paper and roll up the flash paper in my hand. I grab a lighter and take it back to the bar. I show her the paper and then light it. It goes up super quick, almost blowing the eyebrows off her face!

"Holy shit!" she says.

Then I look at her and say, "I'll call you," and walk away.

For me, at the time, that was a big breakthrough because I was doing something that I wouldn't normally do. And she was excited by this approach because no one had obviously done this to her before. It was very fun and a unique way of getting a number. That girl and I never met up in person because I wasn't really bothered about going out with her and I was busy with other girls, but that wasn't the goal at that point. The goal simply was to get in the habit of closing high calibre girls.

Scenarios like this will give you the positive reference of "I can". That's how you get in a habit of closing high calibre women.

"Texting is for flirting or logistics" – Johnny Cassell

Two Ends of the Closing Spectrum

I've chosen to share these two stories because they're two ends of the same spectrum.

The second story is a reference point for going for a number and being playful and creative. When I had that experience, I was happy I was starting to get these techniques into my system. It really boosted my confidence.

At any step in your process, you should acknowledge your positive attempts at doing stuff you would never normally do. If you keep practising, your only limit is your imagination.

That leads us to the first story. The only reason I could instruct my client on how to pick up two girls from the street and take them back home that day was because I had done similar things. I understand from experience how people respond to different situations, and I'm able to guide someone through the process. Even though they've never been through the process themselves, if they trust me, I'm able to get them to their desired destination.

If you want to get numbers from the hot, model-looking girl at your local club or bar, you can do that. If you want to meet a girl on the street, take her for a date there and then, you can do that. If you want to meet a girl and have sex with her the same day, it is very possible. Not all women are going to do that, but if you're thinking in that way and you've got the next step in mind, then you'll be able to take advantage of many opportunities.

I don't think you need a lot more explanation, so unlike the other chapters, we're just going to go straight into the techniques. There's a lot of knowledge I want to share with you and the basic psychology of closing begins and ends at "Just do it".

"If you don't escalate, she doesn't see you as someone she could potentially have sex with" – Johnny Cassell

Techniques:

Open Question Close

The first close is the open question. It's softer and is a good one to use when you want to get used to closing in general. Open questions are gentle because they give the subject the opportunity to give you the information they *want* to give you. Here are some examples of open questions:

- "What's the best way to stay in touch?"
- "How should we continue this conversation?"

Closed questions, on the other hand, have yes/no answers. For example:

- "Can I have your number?"
- "Do you want to go for coffee?"
- "Fancy a date?"

Typically, when asked these questions, you'll get a "No" because the woman's usual pattern is to say "No" when guys ask for her number.

But with open questions, you've given her options. Now you just need to be ready for what is likely to come your way. For example, she may say, "Oh. Facebook", which is fine if you're a social media king, but you also have to think, do you want her to know so much about you so instantly?

It's better to drip feed information, so you can play "the man of mystery". This will have her wanting to find out that next piece of the puzzle every time you meet.

If her response is, "Oh, do you have Facebook?" or "Do you have Instagram?" my response will be, "Oh, come on. We're not 16," or, "You don't honestly think I'm going to share my whole world with you so quickly, right? Don't be silly Give me your phone, and I'll put my number in." Then call your phone from her phone so you've got her number.

A or B Close

Our second close, is what I call the "double bind" or the "A or B". The gist is that you offer two options, both of which result in her giving you her phone number. This is a fantastic technique used in sales. "Do you want the car in blue or the one in red?" If a car salesman asks you that, he's assuming you're buying.

For my A or B, I go with, "Is your number 07 or 075?" This is relative to wherever you live, but you're assuming her number starts one of two prefixes. Once she answers, you can get her to finish off the rest of her number.

The key is to assume you're already getting the number. Assume you're already going to see each other again. If you want to go for an instant date you might even say, "So do you prefer tea or coffee?" "Do you like red or white wine?" or, "Should we go to the pub or the bar?". If you want to see an example of the A or B close, check out my **YouTube channel**.

Instruction Close

It's important that we call this the instruction close because in this close, you are directing them, and people sometimes need to be directed. In the instruction close, you say something like, "Listen, put your number in here, and we can talk about seeing each other again." This language is much more powerful than, "Can I have your number?" because if you ask, you're setting yourself up for a fall.

Remember what I said earlier on: we are all hardwired to say "no". It's comfortable to say "no". If you say, "Can I have your number?" even though they may actually want to see you again, they might still say "no". To completely avoid that, just be more direct and instructional with your closing.

If you're worried about being too aggressive, don't. It's all in your tone of voice. The close needs to feel organic like you've had such a great conversation that it only makes sense to get each other's numbers and see each other again.

Your whole interaction should be joyous and playful. There should be a good vibe going on.

Remember: you want to leave them on a high note. If you let the conversation reach the "Yawn Zone", then that's what they're going to remember when you go for the follow-up. If

you're not getting a call or text back, then more often than not, it's because of where you left them in the conversation.

So when you feel like it's getting exciting, go for that number and have the guts to *tell* them to give it to you.

Closing Tips and Calibration

Different closes work better with different women.
If someone is being hesitant, then you have to be the director. You always want to stay away from using language like "maybe" and "can I?" – "Can I see you again?" "Can I get your number?" "Maybe I can get your number." "Maybe we can meet." Etc. It's too passive. It's servile. With such tentative language, you're demonstrating your uncertainty about obtaining this woman.

She wants you to come from a place of certainty when it comes to that close, but if you're using passive language at the end of your conversation, that suggests you're a man who doesn't believe he can obtain such a woman. That's a clear way to miss an opportunity.

Don't worry about the close seemingly coming out of nowhere.
A lot of people say you need the conversation to naturally flow to the close, but I don't think so. It's very evident what you're there for. If you've effectively gone through the conversation process from Chapter Five, they are already having a compelling conversation, and likely, there's feelings involved. Stimulating conversations are rare, so when they're having one, they're going to want to hold onto that.

So when you're ready to make your move, you can say something like, "I've got to get your number because we're going to have to see each other again," or, "We're going to have to get a drink," or something like that. Those are lines you can use, but what's more important is your tone, and the flirtatious way you make it clear to her you want to see her again.

Make sure *you* get *their* number.
Here's something you need to be aware of as well. She may say, "Oh yeah, okay, I'll take your number," but if you give her *your* number, all you're doing is handing over the follow-up to her, when really, you should be in charge of that.

I feel it's your duty to take the conversation to the next step. You can't hand over your number and think, "Oh maybe she's going to call me." The chances are very slim.

She might be shy. She might have someone in the picture. You just don't know the dynamic. So if she goes, "I'll take your number," say, "Perfect, pass me your phone," then write your number into her phone, then use her phone to call yours right then and there. Every single time I've used this close, it's been met with laughter and a cheeky grin on the woman's face.

The importance of names
Another thing I would suggest is trying to get their full name. If you get their full name, it allows you to do a "background check" on Google, Facebook and/or Instagram. That way you can get a glimpse of their lifestyle and learn a bit about them prior to meeting them the next time.

A friend of mine also does something very clever. He gives the women he meets nicknames. For example, he might call one of them "Geeky" and then his follow-up procedure would just be, "Hey what are you up to, Geeky?"

When she gets a message like that, it puts her back in the place where she met you. For the record, "Hey, what are you up to?" is not a unique message. It's more of a bootie call, but if you add that unique nickname in there, it packs more of a punch.

Sex Closing

Okay, let's say you're in a club and you've had a great conversation. You've been flirting with someone for a majority of the night, and she's been receptive, *really* receptive. What do you do next?

What you need to do first is transition her out of that environment into a place where you can seduce her. My old stand-by? "I'm hungry, let's get something to eat."

If she agrees, you have the option of actually going somewhere to eat, like a late night place or just getting a bottle of wine on the way home. You can jump in a taxi, get that bottle and then go straight to your place and make food. In truth, you might not even make food. You might just get straight to business.

This isn't easy for every guy.

One of my clients I worked with, Rick, was a mentorship client. We really pushed him and pushed him and pushed him. We pushed him to the point where he was picking up incredible women, like the ones pictured in magazines. He was even picking up stewardesses on the plane. It was incredible.

I flew him overseas to Lithuania. He was supposed to be there with these guys for the weekend, but he was having such a great time, I couldn't get him back. He ended up staying there for two weeks. I had to fucking call up the hotel and say,

"Cancel his room." All I saw in his Snapchats every night was him in his hotel room with two hot women at a time.

When we flew him back to London, I said, "Wow, you really cleaned up over there, huh?"

"You know what? No," he said. "I didn't have sex with any of those girls."

"You're kidding me," I said. "It was on a platter."

I realized then that we needed to break this down and figure out why this was happening.

I had Rick write down all of his sexual experiences— whatever they were. Sexual experiences that had turned into long-term relationships. One-night stands. Flings. Whatever. I just wanted him to write down all of the people that he had slept with. Then, we unpacked every single process he had gone through to make those experiences happen.

I was making him conscious of the step-by-step process to get him to that confident state, where A, he had a positive reference and B, he could decide on behaviour to model until he turned it into a habit.

Once we finished this, we put it all into a graph. Then we broke it down into a three-step system. We wrote down all the women he had gotten back to his hotel or his apartment. Then we unpacked the language he had used whilst they were there. Through this process, the pattern became very clear.

Rick would get them to his place, and they'd lie down on his bed and go through each other's Instagram images, building some rapport. Then there would be a transition to a massage and a bit of further escalation there. He would validate her, give her compliments, etc.

Then he would feel so overwhelmed with his feelings, he would say something like "I'd really like to date you".

Right?

Now, that's just too intense for a woman at this stage. He hasn't even kissed her and he's asking her to get emotionally involved. Once you've jumped the gun like that, she definitely isn't going to allow it to get sexual.

Rick's Eilte Three Stage Seduction Process

Stage 1: Build Comfort

What Rick was lacking was the dominance part of male sexuality. So I wrote down three columns, each one representing a step for him to follow. With each column he had a stage of escalation towards sex. The first one might be "Show me your Instagram", or "Show me something about you". This stage is all about sharing things they each care about, building a huge amount of rapport.

Stage 2: Emotional Intimacy

Now it's time to move the interaction into a riskier place and say, "Okay. Right. We're going to play truth or dare." Here the objective is to build even more intimacy, using the rapport you've built to share parts of yourselves you both normally hide from others.

Stage 3: Physical Intimacy

Once the emotional intimacy has been built, it's time to move toward the physical. I would suggest just going in for the kiss and then transitioning into sex, or pinning her down playfully and seeing how she responds and then moving in, or kissing her down the side of her neck.

Other Examples

You may invite her over for a movie, and when you want, verbally escalate by saying something like "I'm just so turned on by you right now". Then go for the kiss and transition to sex.

You might invite them round, then run a bath or have a shower together. Or you could just move close for a cuddle and then transition that into further intimacy.

One thing we did that was fitting for Rick was encourage him to share playlists. You can listen to each other's music (I'd recommend getting a headphone splitter), then transition into a massage, then a kiss, then sex.

If you've got a hotel, get room service. The food and drink will get her relaxed. There's nothing more off-putting than trying to accelerate straight to the physical act of sex. You need a transition. As you're eating or drinking, you can compliment her on something you like about her body, then move in for the kiss and then transition to sex.

Same-day Sex Closing

In terms of having sex on the same day, you've just got to assume it's on. You've got to have the right mindset. You've got to build enough rapport, and you have to create "plausible deniability", especially with younger women.

When you're dealing with older women, you don't really have to deal with that too much. Older women are a bit more liberal, and they know what they want, so you can be more direct with your language. Instead of saying "let's watch a film" (as you would with a younger woman), you should directly state your intent.

But for a girl who's in her early-to-mid 20s, you're dealing with someone who might have a lot of guilt based on society's expectations. So she needs to have "plausible deniability". That means you need to help her dress up the situation so she can dress it up in her own head.

You got to think about what she's going to tell her friends the next day. If you say "Let's go get something to eat", she can tell her friends, "We left the bar to get something to eat, and I don't know, it just happened".

"It just happened" is an easier thing to tell her friends than "Oh yes, he asked if I wanted to go back to his place, so I went back to his place and fucked him". That doesn't allow her to remove any societal guilt from her actions.

Keep things simple. Some basic set-ups are:

- "Let's get something to eat."
- "Let's get out of here. We're going to the after party."
- "Let's go somewhere more interesting."

You could even transition using one of your mutual interests. You can say "I've got to show you this record" earlier in the conversation, and then when you want to leave, bring the topic back up.

How to Deal With Logistics

Typically, I suggest *always* going back to your place. If you have your own place, it's an environment you can absolutely control. Besides, you don't know her situation. You will have to fish for those logistics.

She might be sharing her house with friends. In some cases, she might still live at home with her parents. She might have her own place. These are all things you can find out through conversation. There is an element of suggestion there as well. When you're in a conversation, you can ask, "How many people do you live with?" or, "Which part of town do you live in?". And when she tells you, you can go, "Hmm, okay. Yes, it's not too far," but with a grin on your face like you're implying something. Be ambiguous, but be suggestive.

Remember: you have to assume it's *ON*! You have to lead the seduction. You have to notch up that gear. Very few women will take you to that place. It's up to *you* to make that move. They're waiting…

The Line Between "Suggestive and Cheeky" and "Predatorial and Creepy"

A common concern of my clients when they're trying to sex close is worrying they're coming across as creepy or as "that guy" in the bar. The secret is all about calibration.

Imagine you have two glasses on the table right now and you've got a jug full of water. One of the glasses is called "comfort" and the other "escalation". If you pour too much into one, it's going to overflow. But if you balance it, then you get a balanced state and that's what you're looking to do with your interactions. Strike a balance.

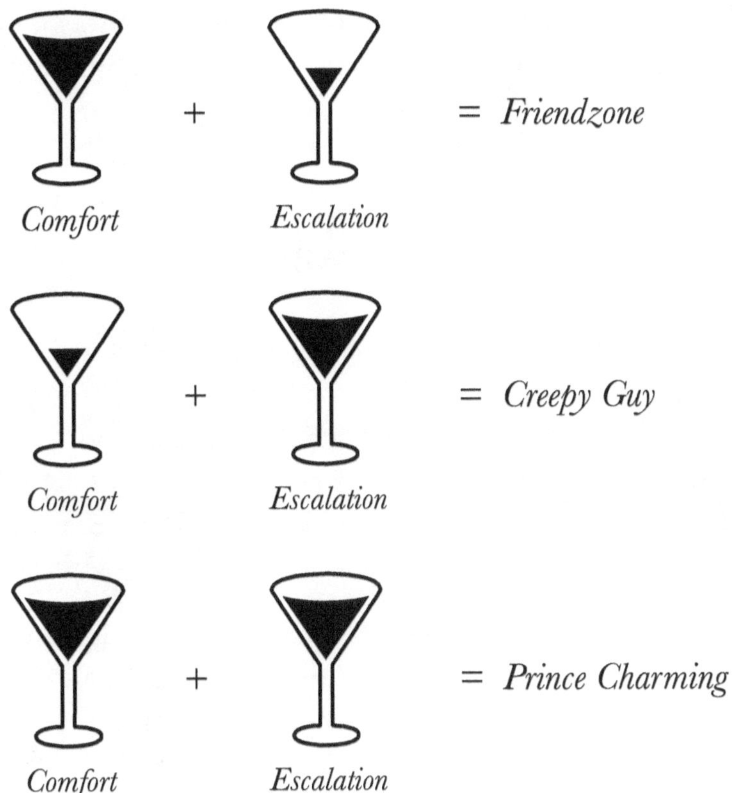

I've been out with another coach and his opener was an instant make out with the girl. He would pull her in and literally make out with her just two seconds after laying eyes on her. She would be like "What the hell?". Then his method was to spend a whole lot of time building comfort because he filled the escalation cup too quickly.

If you go too hard too fast with escalation, people may get freaked out, but if you balance escalation with comfort, you can have a smoother process. The most traditional way is to feel comfort, then escalate. Understand that calibration and play around with it.

This balance between escalation and comfort goes for every step of the process, from your opener to when you finally close that deal for sex.

Takeaways

I want to emphasize that you *need* to get into the habit of closing. Do it now because when you do find that person you really like, this is going to be the one thing you are not going to forget to do.

Now, plan a social event and make it your duty to practise these closing techniques:

- **Instructional close:** Tell them what to do, e.g. "Put your number in here [handing her your phone]."
- **A/B close:** Present two options that have the same conclusion, e.g. "Is it cocktails or prosecco?" or "Are you a texter or a caller?"
- **Open question close:** Ask a question with multiple possible answers, e.g. "What's the best way to stay in touch?"

Finally, closing isn't just about sex. What we're also looking to do is master the art of building platonic relationships to get you access to the people you want to be around, so you can get the things that you want.

Chapter Six: Case Study

Name: Odi
Age: 19
Profession: Business Owner

What areas of your dating world did Johnny work with you on?

Mindset. Johnny helped me realise that it's really how we feel on the inside that's reflected in our interactions with others. A big part was getting over my pessimism and making myself better.

How did working with Johnny on Closing change your life?

I'm not naturally a conversation person but Johnny gave me a basic structure for how a conversation should happen.

Once I had the structure, I could go out and practise it over and over and try new things.

The base structure then evolves and you can add a bit of humour here and there and have fun with the conversations, safe in the knowledge that you've got something to fall back on should there be a conversational lull.

Which of the techniques that Johnny taught you do you still use on a regular basis?

I used to get jealous when I saw couples. Johnny told me something along the lines of "that's a great thing, go and try to interact with them and learn more from them".

Now I never get jealous of anything, I just get fun and think "Wow, that's great for you guys, congratulations!".

How did working with Johnny help you outside of the dating world?

I have to do a lot of presentations and he's helped me with my base confidence and interactions with big groups of people.

What was the most valuable lesson Johnny taught you?

I was quite a sexual guy but I value being kind and generous more, so I was coming off as the "nice guy" so he helped me inject some sexual escalation into the conversation. This meant that women saw me as someone that they could fool around with.

To learn more about constructing your Elite Seduction lifestyle, head over to *www.JohnnyCassell.com/BookResources*, where you'll find exclusive techniques and access to the **'5 Seduction Secrets High-Class Women Wish You Knew'**.

Building Social Wealth

"You're not going out to pick up. You're going out to meet cool, interesting people." – Johnny Cassell

---

Back when I was "going out with the lads", there was a certain level of social value, but it was limited to my friends of convenience. These were the people I went to school with, and who I had bonded with. It was comfortable, but it wasn't giving me access to the things I wanted from life.

As I've made clear earlier in this book, your social circle is directly connected to how successful you'll be in any area of your life. In this chapter, I will take you back to the beginning of my social life, when I was at school. I will show you how I created a social network on the playground and how I used that as a template for massive success in the Reading (the town I grew up in) nightlife scene.

What you'll learn from this chapter is how to build effective social circles and create a strategy for forming those relationships.

We're not talking about women in this chapter. We're talking about how to build your social value in general, and not just in your local town or city. I took this same model and brought it to London and now effectively use it on a global scale. And what in the past took me a couple of months to do, I'm now able do in three days.

Story: The Merging of the Tribes

When I was an awkward 15-year-old still in school, there was nothing to do. I'd ask for some money from my parents to "go to the cinema", but really, I would chip in with my friends to go and buy a big crate of booze and get pissed in a field.

In Reading, there wasn't much going on, except for those under 18 parties that popped up every now and again. I dreamt of throwing my own parties, but I needed *everyone* to come, so I decided to change the way I behaved in the playground.

I had my own social group, but every break and lunch time I would walk round the playground and join other social groups: the sporty kids kicking the football around, the geeks with their GameBoys, the naughty kids at the bottom of the playground smoking cigarettes, the greebos listening to their music. Different pockets of people.

I'd go round to each social group and create genuine connections with these people, and over time, I was able to create a diverse group of school friends.

I realised there were talented people in each of the different social groups. One of my friends (in the sporty crowd) was really into his dance music and was a DJ. Another friend (in the greebo crowd) was a drum and bass DJ.

With all these DJs in hand, I decided to throw my party.

I got a bunch of soft drinks and a lot of booze and put together a schedule for the DJs and some bands. I wanted the event to appeal to all my different friends, so they all had something to listen to.

The event was a huge success because I had already built all the relationships. This also made our year group unique. With most year groups, there were those typical cultural divides, but my events enabled our class to bond.

After the events, I had loads of leftover soft drinks (of course all of the booze was consumed), and I thought, "Fuck, what am I going to do with these?" So, I filled up my sports bag, took them to school, and did the same route around the playground I did everyday day, selling the cans for £1 each. I made a killing, and I thought, "Holy shit, I'm onto something here."

I had a contact at the *Mars Factory* in Slough (the neighbouring city), so I bought boxes and boxes of chocolate and went to wholesalers to buy more crates of Coke. With my sports bag full, I walked the same route each day.

I ended up putting the tuck shop out of business because I was going straight to the consumer. I was so busy I had to employ one of my friends.

All of that was built on relationships, but what I was unconscious of at the time was how the social wealth I had built in the playground allowed me to create two successful businesses at a young age.

Once you master relationships, you can do *anything*. Once I realized what I had done in the playground, I took that model into the Reading nightlife, and in a short time, I knew pretty much everyone: managers, door staff, anyone who had weight in that scene.

When a club is completely packed, and they're not letting anyone in, if you've got a relationship with someone at the door, you will be the exception. And if you've got a relationship with the managers of certain establishments, it can add rocket fuel to your night and boost the experience for your friends, along with your reputation. You're going to get treated differently, and it will affect every area of your life.

Story: How to Become an Instant Celebrity

So how do I do this in three days? Well, follow me to Lithuania.

I went on a trip to Lithuania with a client, but we were only going for a weekend. Still, while I was there, I wanted to see if I could duplicate my experiences from Reading and London.

Conventionally what happens when you go away, you fall into the tourist trap. However, I'm a firm believer in the law of association, and I wanted to hack the high-end scene. So on the first day in Vilnius, we made our rounds to all of the high-end stores to collect data.

At each place, we asked the same sort of questions: "Where's the best place to go?" "Which clubs are the best?" "Who has the best the table service?" etc. We went to Burberry, Prada, Dior, and similar places because they all had one thing in common: the workers appreciated the finer things in life. For them to refer a shitty place to a new client of theirs is not a great reflection of their brand. It's in their best interest to refer

me to something that they feel is an extension of that high-end culture.

We got the data (thank you, Karolina and Ruta), went to the hotel concierge and got him to book us a table at the *Materialist,* one of the top clubs in Vilnius. Now there was a bit of expense involved, but we weren't going out to get drunk. We were looking beyond that. We were paying to get close to key individuals. As such. we were given a few price options for tables: from €100 to €300. €300 split between us got us the best table in the club, with our own private security guard right next to the DJ.

Once we claimed that space, I made sure I number closed everyone. I closed people at the table next to us. I closed the DJ, thanking him for the music, and asking him what track he was playing. Then I asked him for some suggestions for Saturday and even Sunday night. The DJ turned out to be one of our most important contacts. He had all the insider info.

Sunday night he told me was the *biggest* fashion show of the year. He told us where we could get tickets, but he also told us where the after-party was. We got the tickets (second row from the front), and when we got there, we saw the most astonishing looking models you can imagine.

From there, all I had on my mind was getting into the after-party. So we made our move, talking to the others in the front rows until we got the invite. An hour later, we were at the after-party with the designer, the models, the PR team, and all the local restaurateurs and nightclub owners. We had the whole town in our back pocket from that one trip and it only took *three* days.

We grew such a great rapport with these guys that they invited us back for a new club launch, a private party, and a special event. Now, every time we go back to Lithaunia, we're treated like royalty because we treat them the same way.

When you establish key contacts, it's important to first of all identify they are in fact a key contact, then bring them in close and offer them value. That means doing things like remembering their birthday, and if it's your second visit, you always come with a gift. If you invest in those relationships, they will pay dividends.

Of course, you can't always replicate that exact model, but what you can replicate is how proactive you are in accumulating data, how you behave and how you treat those relationships over time.

---

*"You are **never** missing out on the party if you **are** the party"* – Johnny Cassell

---

Playground Dynamism

These two stories illustrate how, even when you're in two very different environments, you can apply the same skillset to great effect.

When you get access to different social circles, you gain a new perspective. You get access to events, people, and situations you'd normally never know about. The same is true with international friends. When you bother to learn about someone else's culture or someone else's upbringing or language, they will recognise you as someone who is different, someone who doesn't fit the general consensus. They'll recognise you as unique and that's a pattern of behaviour you should look to adopt and make part of your self-development.

Always look to go into unknown territories and so you can grow your circle. No matter how high up the social tree you climb, the principles are going to be the same. In essence, the rules of the playground, they do not change.

The reason my social circle expands quickly is because these highly influential people have executed a similar strategy during their climb. If they moved to a new city, that was an ambitious thing, and to thrive, they had to meet people quickly.

Understand that no one really knows anyone and everyone is in the same boat. Effectively it's your first day at school again, where it's only beneficial for you to be the most social so you can build your friendship base.

Humans are wired to be drawn towards the most "pre-selected" people. Pre-selected is the principle that if everyone else is attracted to you, you must be attractive. If you don't demonstrate that through women who find you attractive, then you can demonstrate that through the social wealth you've built.

Imagine this. You walk into a nightclub, and you've got rapport with the door guy, you've got rapport with the girl taking your coat. You know the event manager, the owner, the DJ, the bar girl, and everyone seems to be giving you attention.

You see a friend in there who's having an office party. He introduces you to his group of friends. Suddenly the women in the room see you as someone at the centre of that environment.

They've seen what you're wearing and who you're with, how you're going about your business and they're left thinking, "Who the fuck is that guy, and why don't I know him?".

This is how you invoke the power of "familiarity by association". If you meet a woman because she's introduced to you by a mutual friend, it offers a degree of comfort knowing you've already been selected by people close to her. Her walls come down as her curiosity rises and attracting her becomes effortless.

"Break the pattern of what people normally expect"
– Johnny Cassell

Techniques:

The Social Snowball

The social snowball is a concept I came up with many years ago, and it's all to do with how you invest your time and leverage your contacts. I'm going to highlight the social snowball's effectiveness with a story:

When I was still living in Reading, I was watching a friend's Indie-rock band, *Vices*, play at a pub called the Oakford. Afterwards, everyone just wanted to sit around and speak with the guys and do that "we're-hanging-with-the-band-so-we-must-be-cool" thing. I was with my wingman, and I looked at him and said, "Fuck this, man, let's get out of here."

We bounce over to some commercial place called Vodka Revolution and the queue is backed up as far you can see, so I just walk straight up to the door because I have rapport with the bouncer, and my buddy and I walk straight in. This gets immediately acknowledged by everyone who's been trying to get in for the last half hour.

I go over to the bar and order myself an obscure drink – a pint of milk or something silly like that. I see my friend who is having an office party and I go over and he introduces me to his friends before my friend and I head to the dance

floor, where we commence taking the piss out of each other. We're just throwing some silly Michael Jackson kicks at each other and having a good time, and I say, "Listen, I'll bet you anything, in 10 seconds some women are going to come over." He agrees, and I count to 10 seconds and sure as hell, a group of women shows up next to us.

I'm not surprised because we're two guys having fun, not two creeps looking for a cheap grind, and women are attracted to guys who know how to have fun. We take the piss out of the way these women dance, and they take the piss out of us for a little bit. Then my friend goes to the loo, and as I'm bobbing my head to the beat, taking my time coming off the dance floor, this petite little brunette suddenly shows up right in the centre.

She comes out of nowhere and she's flashing her eyes like full-beam headlights at me.

"Where the fuck did she come from?" I think. I take my eyes off her and put them back, and she's still beaming at me. It's really *on* now.

"How've you been?" I mouth to her.

This forces an indicator from her. "What?" she mouths back.

"Come here," I respond and meet her halfway before I ask, "How've you been?"

"Yeah, I've been good," she says.

I've never met this girl in my life, but I say, "Oh, I haven't seen you in a long time."

"Yeah, yeah. I work—" she says, and she talks about this other bar where she works.

"Funny," I say, "because I've got all of your friend's numbers but not yours. Why is that?"

"Oh, I don't know," she says.

Then I say, "Listen, why are you pretending to know me?"

"What?" she asks.

"I know what you're trying to do," I respond then grab her hand, move her off the dance floor, and sit her down.

It took me less than five minutes to leave with that girl. My poor friend is in the toilet, and when he comes out, I'm gone. I woke up at her place the next day thinking, "How the fuck did that just happen? How did I get her in five minutes?"

But in reality, it didn't take me five minutes. I had been investing in that five minutes for close to an hour. The hour consisted of me demonstrating my social value, skipping the whole queue, minding my own business, mingling with those I did know and just sparking people's intrigue. She had been watching and waiting for her opportunity to show interest.

This is the power of the social snowball. Here's how you build your own:

The Bouncer

The first step is breaking the pattern of how you interact with the guy working the door at a nightclub or bar. Think about the pattern they're used to. Typically, they ask the guy to show some ID and then decide whether they're going to let him in. It's up to you to break that expected pattern.

When I approach a new bouncer at an exclusive club, I go up to the guy and say something like, "I bet you've lost count of how many girls you've slept with in this place."

He'll either say, "Yeah, it's quite a lot" or "Ah, it's not really like that".

To be honest, I don't really care about his response. I just want any response. That way I can introduce myself and find out his name.

Once you've got that name, you put it in your phone and you make a note of where you met him. The next week when you go there, he's going to recognise you but he's not going to remember

your name. That's okay. You remember his name and be sure you use it, and when you do, he will feel obliged to learn yours.

Remember this: it's very difficult to be an asshole to someone who's being nice. So feed that ego and get that relationship in your back pocket.

The Till Girl/Coat Check

The next person you will likely come across at the club will be the till girl (might be a guy, but that's unlikely). You can compliment her on something she's wearing, but again, the whole point is to get her name. She may not remember your name the first week, but the second week, she'll feel obliged. The same concept here applies: give value and get a name.

The Bar Tender

Did you notice the drink I ordered in my story? There's a reason it was so obscure. I want to break the pattern of bartenders getting normal drink orders from nameless people at the bar. I also want to know their name.

I tip them as well. You've got to tip because that pays dividends later. Say you've met a woman and you want to get to a bar that's eight people deep. Because you've tipped, you've got direct access. It's a great subtle display of value.

The DJ

The DJ, you can easily compliment him on his track or his music and give him a high-five. You can mention to him how that track "was such a banger Shazam didn't even pick it up" or some other gushing compliment.

The point again is to get his name, but why not take it one step further? Why don't you go to the bar and get that guy a drink? He's been stuck behind that booth all night!

Same can be said for the bouncers or the VIP doorman. You can go to the bar and slip a couple of soft drinks or Red Bulls in their pocket. No one ever thinks about doing this. No one gives a shit about these people. They just see them as part of the environment. If you start seeing them as people and building a rapport with them, then it's going to pay dividends.

PR/Event Management

These same principles apply to the people in PR, the event managers. These are the folks on the streets giving out flyers and getting people to come to their bar. If you can't identify these people, then simply ask the people you do have relationships with who they are so you can approach them. Give them props for putting on a great night, and mention how your friends keep coming every week because they've got their parties down to a T. Again, get their name and number.

In night-life, just like in every industry, everyone knows each other. When you get to know the managers and the event staff, they may introduce you to the owners of a neighbouring club. Can you see how quickly this can snowball? And if you're building social circles outside of your industry circles, you can leverage them against each other.

For example, you might know a girl who has 10 hot friends, and if she wants to throw a party, you can use that as an opportunity to give back to the environment you've built a relationship with. You say to the girls, "Let me handle this, I want to make sure you have the best night imaginable." Then you call up your buddy at the club and tell him, "I've got 10 coming to the club for a special night. Will we be able to do something for them?"

The way I see it, you're doing these guys a favour. After all, it's their job to bring attractive women to the club so the men spend more money. Always be thinking about the big picture.

Exercise: Create Your Own Social Snowball

Here's a step-by-step guide to creating your own social snowball:

1. Write a list of the places you think will yield the calibre of women you want to be around.
2. Draft out the hierarchy of key players (you can use the list above) at that venue.
3. Now your job is to put a name and number to every one of those people.
4. Using the techniques in this section, develop rapport with these people and make them your friends.

If you follow this plan of action and build those relationships, you'll go from "some guy" in the club to "that guy" in the club. And if you extend these techniques outside your dating life, you can quickly meet highly influential people.

Social Media Wealth

It's shocking how social media is still one of the most misunderstood tools you have in your possession, but Facebook became very instrumental to how I met my current girlfriend. More about that later.

If you are becoming skilled at building relationships on a national and international level, then you need a tool that can successfully manage those relationships, and Facebook is exactly that. I wouldn't normally recommend people getting on

Facebook at the early stages, but with international cases it's to your advantage to do so; otherwise, it's just going to become a lost number in your address book later forgotten.

Facebook gives you access to events (one of the most overlooked features), and it gives you a record of your key contacts' birthdays. Birthdays are something you need to keep up with if you're going to nurture your relationships with the key influencers of your various social circles.

Facebook is also a platform for you to showcase your brand. And in posting content, you need to follow Maslow's hierarchy of needs. Ask yourself, does my content convey that I can offer security? Does it convey that I have high self-esteem or have reached some form of actualization? If you simplify your profile and focus on your core values and Maslow's principles, you are on your way to developing your brand.

Another thing you can do on Facebook is what I call the "social photo joint venture", and I have some great friends who do really well at this. They strategically take photos with people who have a similar size Facebook followings and share those images on their timelines so they can expose each other to each other's audiences.

If you want to look at someone that does this tremendously well, check out a friend of mine, Julius Dein. He creates prankster and magic videos and shares his content on people's pages who have a similar-sized audiences. He recently just hit nine million followers. This guy now can get paid anywhere from £45,000 to £100,000 to be flown out somewhere just to do a few Snapchats and a video.

As you can see, social media has the potential to create attraction through close circles in your proximity and create buzz on a much grander scale.

How to Be a Social Media King

First of all, you need to recognise yourself as a brand. And as such, you've got to think about your audience. Think of it this way: When someone looks at your profile page, they're looking through your shop window. Does what you're showcasing demonstrate value?

Images you post need to go through some kind of quality control, so don't just automatically accept images you're tagged in. There needs to be a grooming process.

What you want to convey is a lifestyle. That doesn't mean a pic that says "Here's my brand new Ferrari". No one cares about that. What people care about are your values. If you like travelling, then a picture of you experiencing a new culture is a great picture to post. Try to avoid clichés like the Hollywood sign or the fucking Eiffel Tower. Also, no one needs to see you with your top off.

Get rid of all of your university pictures of you pissed up on Freshers' Week. That's certainly not sexy. Everyone goes out and gets pissed. It doesn't need to be part of your brand.

Having pictures with your friends is great, but make sure you are in the middle. You don't want people to come to your page and then get side-tracked, looking at all of your other friends' pages. You want them to come to your shop so they can buy your brand. So stop advertising someone else's.

Data Management

As you begin building your social snowball, you will quickly build up a tremendous amount of data, and this data is going to be useless if you don't manage it correctly.

In the early days, when I met someone who I felt was a key contact, I would get out my phone, enter their name and the brand or company or club they were associated with and maybe a little description. Then I'd go home and put all the new places and people into an A4 pad so I could keep track.

Since then, my way of managing data has become much more sophisticated. Now, I simply use a spreadsheet with simple columns:

- Name
- Phone number
- Email
- Description
- Notes

That's it. Just those simple columns, along with extra tabs for the cities or countries where these people live. Now, when I collect the data into my phone, I make sure to put it straight into my spreadsheet when I get home. I use Google Sheets. It's available on any device you can connect to the Internet. The key thing is to record the data; otherwise, it's going to get lost in your phone or simply be forgotten.

My girlfriend's whole first year of business was based on the contacts she accumulated over the years. She had £50,000 worth of debt and in her first year, she cleared the £50,000, made a profit, and acquired a free office, just by using her network.

When I think about all the things that have come my way, it's all through relationships and contacts. We all have the power to do this, but a lot of us fall short because we don't know how to manage our data properly.

How to Manage Your Social Relationships

Maintaining relationships is all about providing value, so always be thinking of how you can add value to other people's lives before you take value.

Imagine you have a relationship with a fitness instructor, who you know teaches a lot of hot, successful women on a one-to-one basis, and for his birthday, he's inviting all his clients out to celebrate, and he's given you a plus one.

Now, if you know someone who is single and from a social circle you'd like to get more acquainted with, then you can invite him to the party, therefore providing him value. After all, guys always appreciate being introduced to hot women. That is a universal law.

You can even go as far as creating your own event. If you've built a relationship at your favourite restaurant and there's a great sushi chef there, you can host a house party and get that chef to come to your house for a sushi-making master class with all your buddies. Then invite the people who you think would benefit from meeting each other during such an evening.

You have to become the reason people are getting to know each other and making things happen, the reason people are meeting their partners and finding love. The more people see you as a connector, the more value will come your way.

Takeaways

As you can see, the social snowball is an incredibly powerful tool to help you become the person you want to be. With it, you'll have women trying to seduce *you*, and through it, you'll gain the essential skills you need to start your own business or realise goals in other areas of your life.

- **Invest in yourself:** Think about how you position yourself. Buying VIP tickets can massively increase how others perceive you.
- **Pre-select yourself:** If you know the key players in a scene, you become "pre-selected", meaning the more others like you, the more people will be drawn to you
- **Show your best side on social media:** Your Facebook profile is a demonstration of your personal brand. Make sure when people look at it, they immediately understand your values.
- **Sort your data:** You need to make sure you keep all the data you acquire. Use *Google Sheets* to build a spreadsheet of everyone you meet.
- **Provide value:** From buying drinks for the bouncers to connecting club owners with groups of hot women, you've got to put helping others at the forefront of your mind. Put yourself in their shoes and ask yourself "What would I want?".

Chapter Seven: Case Study

Name: Jaye
Age: 25
Profession: Business Owner

What areas of your dating world did Johnny work with you on?

Approaching women, leading them and keeping them invested.

How did working with Johnny on Building Up Your Network change your life?

It gave me access to more opportunities with not only women, but useful contacts and business opportunities.

Which of the techniques that Johnny taught you do you still use on a regular basis?

Mindsets, pacing conversations, leading and relationship investment strategies.

How did working with Johnny help you outside of the dating world?

It has not only helped me become a more social and attractive man, but he has enabled me to live life fearlessly.

What was the most valuable lesson Johnny taught you?

No "what ifs", always try something or approach someone if you are interested because it's better to fail and learn from your mistakes than not even give yourself that chance.

For more resources and access to **'5 Seduction Secrets High-Class Women WISH you knew'**, head over to *www.JohnnyCassell.com/BookResources*

CHAPTER EIGHT:
Communicating Love

"If you don't learn to communicate your feelings toward your partner, they'll end up communicating them with someone else" – Johnny Cassell

---

For most men, understanding the language women speak is like trying to read gibberish. In reality, it's about being able to communicate on an emotional level. This is something that, I confess, was a huge breakthrough for me. It's still something I actively work on today.

What you'll gain from this chapter is the ability to communicate to your partner that you care for them on a deep, emotional level. I'm not talking about words. Actions speak louder than words.

Saying to your partner that you love her, taking her to dinner or spending the night at a hotel, these are just normal things. They don't have the romantic punch you might think. What I want you guys to learn is how to dress these experiences

up so they're unique enough to elicit an emotional response from your partner.

The seduction community tends to focus on just picking up the girl because it grooms the ego. To be honest, picking up a girl and even having sex with her isn't difficult. What's difficult and what transitions you from a boy to a man is when you can support and provide for your partner in a loving relationship.

A lot of people aren't talking about this stuff because they're too caught up in the instant gratification of getting a number or having same-day sex. Don't get me wrong, those things *do* have value, and if you don't do them, you're probably going to always wish you had.

But get it out of your system. Build self-esteem and confidence through meeting a selection of women, understand the different flavours out there and what your needs are, so you can determine what you want. Then, when you do find the one you want, learn how to respond to her emotional needs so you can maintain the relationship.

The truth is, among all the people who teach you how to pick up women, few have experienced long-term relationships. That's because they never reconditioned their behaviour around women.

For most of your life, you've conditioned yourself to respond to women in certain social environments by acting on it or punishing yourself for not acting on it. But the first step of reconditioning yourself for a real relationship is actively saying to everyone, "I've got a girlfriend now. I'm done."

As we spoke about before, your thoughts are your perception. If you're still in the mindest of picking-up women and wanting multiple partners, you will continue to live in that world and find it near impossible to have a succesful long-term partner.

Reconditioning yourself is about changing the lens that you view the world through and actively evolving how you approach and interact with social situations.

Story: Unleashing My Inner Romantic

When I was younger, I met this girl. She was caring, family orientated, and very passive. I thought she was incredible, and that she would add some stability to my otherwise choatic life. But at that time of my life, I had one objective and that was simply to teach seduction. That is what I wanted to do. It was my life's mission.

In order for me to have any credibility teaching people these skills, I had to be constantly experiencing women. So, when I met this girl, I said to her, "Look, this is the way it is. It's where my life is going, and that's why I can't have a relationship." But she said, "It doesn't have to be like that."

So we discussed having an open relationship, where I could be out most nights meeting women either alone or with my clients. I'd go out for drinks, sleep with women, whatever.

At the time, it was a relationship model that worked for both of us, and even though I was with other women, I still added value to that relationship by being respectful to the boundaries we had agreed upon. However, despite the relationship and all my socializing, I still hadn't developed my emotional empathy. I hadn't mastered the ability to romance a woman. I appreciate the irony.

I had mastered the ability to meet, attract, and seduce women, but I hadn't learned how to develop a real romantic

connection. The issue became apparent to me when my girlfriend and I hadn't gone away for some time.

It was her mother and brother-in-law who strongly encouraged our trip to Paris. When they made the suggestion, I was like, "Yes, absolutely. I should do that. That would be great." And it was. We had a fantastic time and made some fun memories.

A succesful relationship is about experiencing moments together, but if we get too caught up with our daily goals and tasks, we forget to dedicate time to our nearest and dearest. We become too selfish. During my entire relationship, I was so caught up with my own personal goals that the entire relationship became about me. I only thought inwardly about Johnny and not enough about the people around me.

Looking back, I feel annoyed at myself. "Why wasn't I thinking like that? Why did I never think that was a good idea?" If I'm being honest with myself, it is because I was too wrapped up in my work. I kept it as a priority day and night instead of doing what I could to nurture my relationship.

In the end, that relationship fell apart for other reasons, but it was still a big eye opener for me looking back, realising, "Shit, this is the next ceiling I need to break through. I need to really work on this".

Story: Romantic Released!

Even though I'm a dating coach, I'll admit I don't have the perfect relationship. The perfect relationship does not exist. What you're looking for is *compatibility*. Even in my recent relationships, I've been told off from time to time for not being the planner, or not doing romantic gestures.

If you're dating a passive woman, you won't even know you're doing anything wrong. Then suddenly one day, you'll break up and you won't even know why. But it's because you've lost their respect. So what I value in my relationship now is a woman who challenges me. If you're dating a challenging woman, she won't be passive about the situation. She'll let you know when you need to do more.

As I said, I go through periods where I'm so engrossed in my work, I don't take care of nurturing my relationship. I did the same thing with a recent girlfriend. So, to make up for it, I decided to do something special.

I planned a trip to Edinburgh for her birthday.

Here's the thing: Anyone can book a night in a hotel or a fancy restaurant. That's normal. What matters is how you dress it up. When I booked a trip to Edinburgh, I asked myself two questions: "How can I make this more unique?" "How can I make it more personal?"

So I went through all of her Instagram and Facebook pictures and the personal pictures we had on our computer and compiled them into one album. There were images of her and her set of friends, her and her family, me and her on our adventures and us together at certain stages of our life. Then, I found an app that could print them in a Polaroid format.

I had all the prints sent to my address. Then I called the hotel and I told them to make sure there was pecan pie in the room upon our arrival (it was around Thanksgiving time and she, being American, missed the holiday). I also told them to put rose petals all around the room. Finally, I told them to expect a package of Polaroids and that I would like them to scatter the images around the room.

When you challenge yourself to be creative with romance, you can end up surprising yourself with what you come up with. That little bit of effort made a huge difference in our relationship. With that gesture, I was separating myself from being a guy just doing the run of the mill into a man doing something truly unique and personal. That trip to Edinburgh is not something someone else is going to be able to replicate.

"Be aware of the words you choose to describe your situation as it actually forms the reality you live in" - Johnny Cassell

---

Emotional Availability

You need to calibrate your emotional availability based on the other person. No straight woman wants to be with a man who is too free with his emotions – it's like dating a woman.

Imagine taking care of a child, who makes every emotional issue they have your problem. Does this fill you with confidence about the child's stability or does it frustrate you? Emotional availability is the same. Feel free to share your fears, anxieties, and worries, but don't make them your partner's problem. Women are looking for men to be genuine, but they're not looking to deal with another's person baggage.

Still, it's important to speak on an emotional level – to express your feelings about particular issues in the relationship, including how you feel towards your partner. On that note, if someone is close to you, and you've never told them you love them, that's something that you need to do.

Sometimes you will need to express negative emotions. That's okay. If you're angry, show you're angry, and be clear when something doesn't align with your values to prevent yourself from becoming angry later.

Healthy relationships come from effective communication, and they break down when people aren't communicating. Let's say one partner fears expressing a certain feeling or issue in their relationship. If they don't express that feeling, then it will become a bigger problem later. So, whether what you need to express is positive or negative, you need to be firm and feel reassured that the relationship will get stronger when you open up that dialogue. You have to allow yourself to feel vulnerable through expressing your feelings. If you fail to do so, it's just going to come back to haunt you later.

Brace Yourself for the Shift

Women like to test men. So if you're trying to make that girl you're seeing your exclusive girlfriend, she is going to test you. The most common test is that she'll tell you she's breaking it off just to see how you respond. At this moment, most guys panic, and think, "Oh, shit. Well, it's over, oh okay." But that is the moment you need to act!

You need to understand where this is coming from. She's realising, "Oh my God. I'm getting feelings for this guy. I'm starting to emotionally invest. But I'm not sure he's quite there yet, so what I'm going to do is just call it off because I don't want to get hurt. I don't think he's serious enough." Again, you're not communicating with each other, but let me be clear, if she behaves like this, she's not really breaking it off.

What she's basically trying to communicate to you is, "Show me you care. Show me you're interested in me."

When I started dating my current girlfriend, we didn't even kiss each other for about a month. Still, we knew we were on the same page. The emotional investment was getting there.

So I decided to take her out of the bubble of London on a road trip down to Oxford. We had a lovely day out.

On the way back, I had to pop into my family home to pick up a shirt because I had a friend's birthday to go to that night in London. I said, "Look, I have to pop in, but you're not seeing my mum just yet."

"Yes, I'm coming in," she says. "I'm going to meet your mom."

"No, you're not," I respond. "You're going to sit in the car and wait, and then we'll go."

For me, it was ridiculous for her to meet my mum so soon. I wanted to take our relationship slowly, and meeting the parents is a relationship rite of passage I wasn't planning to let happen for a long while.

I pull up to my drive. She jumps out of the car, barges her way in to my house, and introduces herself to my mum. My mum doesn't know what's hit her. She's never met this girl in her life. Still, she met my mum, and after that meeting, I had a feeling that this relationship could be something special. I also realised I should tell my girlfriend more about my unique profession.

At this stage, my girlfriend hadn't seen a lot of my videos or read my content. *You guys have it easy!* For a woman, dating a dating coach is a lot like dating a stripper. When I go out, I have to speak to women. It's part of my job. So imagine if I'm half an hour late. My girlfriend is going to wonder, "Why is he half an hour late? What's he been up to?"

The reality is, I'm not up to anything, but I need to qualify someone who is emotionally mature enough to handle a relationship like that. That was what I needed to screen her on. So I took her up to my childhood bedroom (now converted into an office) showed her some of my videos and observed how she responded to them and for those of you that have visited my YouTube channel, you know what's on them.

"Oh, okay," she said. "Well, I don't know about that. I don't know if I need this in my life."

When those words fell on my ears, I was disheartened. All I could say was, "What? Okay. Whatever, this is who I am. This is what I do."

We jumped in the car and hit the road back to London. We did not talk throughout the entire journey. Just before we got back to London, I had had enough and I said, "You know what? Fuck it, I don't even care what you think. What I know is that I fucking like you, and that's what matters."

In that moment, she turned around and jumped over the centre console of the car and kissed me. That was our first kiss! I'm still driving the fucking car, and she just goes for it. That's when I realized she had been testing me to see if I was going to be emotionally available – to see if I could demonstrate to her that I *actually* liked her and, if I did, at what level.

She didn't give a fuck about the videos. She just needed that reassurance, and she saw an opportunity to test me. Most men wouldn't even see that. They would just think, "Well, fuck it then," and not feel secure enough to demonstrate their feelings. But by misunderstanding their woman's cue and not acting on it, they miss out on something real.

"Uncertainity at the beginning is exciting. Throughout is detrimental." – Johnny Cassell

---

Techniques:

How to Start Giving a Shit

Men typically don't have a natural knack for emotional language. I personally don't have too many references for it myself. Growing up, no one in my life really communicated that way with me, so emotional communication was not something I adopted from my family.

If you're in a similar position, and you're looking to start gaining that reference, my best advice is to listen to your body.

Try this the next time you're out. When you walk past something and you get a little sliver of inspiration, do something about it! You may see something in a shop window or an upcoming event, and in your mind you may think, "Oh, my girlfriend would like that." Or you may hear a song and think, "Oh, that reminds me of so and so."

Everyone can relate to those moments, but most people let them pass. But that tiny moment is the difference between you giving a shit and you not giving a shit.

So start giving a shit. Start doing more of the things that matter. That's how you will communicate to your woman you are thinking about her.

Just today I walked past a flower shop and I realised I hadn't put fresh flowers in the new apartment since I moved in. That's an example of what I'm talking about. It's these things, these ideas you need to recognise and act on.

If you don't, then later, they will creep up on you and become part of a negative campaign of regret you inflict on yourself. You could have done all these things but you didn't.

And when it comes to how you feel about your partner, this inaction expresses one thing – that you don't really give a shit.

Exercise: How to Give a Shit

We briefly touched on this in the last chapter but take a moment and imagine yourself in the shoes of someone you love or respect.

1. Write down five people you care for.
2. Underneath each name, write down three things you could do for them that would bring value to their lives.
3. Start doing those things.

This might mean cooking dinner for your mum, it might mean sending a bottle of wine to a close friend you haven't seen in a while, it might even be sending a postcard to an elderly relative. The goal here is to find ways to provide value to others and get your head out of the "me-me-me" mindset.

Paying Back Emotional debt

One of the best ways to get in touch with your vulnerability and learn how to communicate on an emotional level is to start paying back emotional debt. Emotional debt gets built up every time we don't talk to someone about how we're feeling, whether we are happy, sad, angry, or grateful.

Confronting people is uncomfortable, but by paying off that emotional debt, you will begin to realize that people don't hate you and will in fact accept you.

By expressing your emotions you become more honest, and once you start becoming more honest with yourself, it becomes much easier to be vulnerable around someone you'd like to keep in your life long-term.

One of my clients is the CEO of a big Fintech company. Though he was successful in his career, he had issues demonstrating his feelings towards his girlfriend. It was actually his girlfriend at the time who approached me to help fix their relationship.

What we came up with was this idea of resolving all of his emotional debt. I found out he had never told his girlfriend he loved her. We also found out he had never really demonstrated affection and love towards his parents, or at least gratitude. This snowballed into other realizations: that he didn't really know his own sister, and that he spent a lot of his time being selfish and focused on himself. These were the kind of things we needed to highlight and address.

We made a list of all the people he wanted to show love and gratitude toward but never had. One by one, he started taking steps towards expressing that gratitude. He invited his mum out for coffee and had a great day. And as he sat there with his mum, he said, "I never really told you how much I love you, Mum. For me, it's important you know that."

That's a big thing.

It's a big thing that a lot of us think to say but we never do because we've never seen that sort of affection demonstrated in our own family. For us, showing that sort of affection seems unusual.

It's not. It's the right thing to do.

In terms of his sister, we started with some weekend activities. They went to a "secret cinema" event together and then built up to other more elaborate experiences until they eventually went together on a holiday.

These were positive changes, but we didn't rest there. We dug deeper so we could understand why he had been like this in the first place. We discovered that when he was in primary school, there was a girl he liked. She ran a competition between two guys (one was him), telling them she would date whichever guy could leave the best voice mail message.

At the time, my client was very young and emotionally open, so he allowed himself to be vulnerable and express those eight-year-old emotions over that voicemail. To his humiliation, when she received the voicemail, she shared it with everyone in the playground. He was now the laughing stock of the whole school, and he didn't even get the girl. She went with the guy who was just a closed up jackass.

That became his reference: "If I demonstrate my emotions, I will be punished," and that was the reason why he was so emotionally closed off throughout his life. That early childhood memory planted a strong negative seed preventing him from being vulnerable.

We are a combination of the people around us. There's a lot of events in our life we hold onto that shape our everyday reality. We all have something that is holding us back. We need to take stock of those things and find a way to move past them by paying our emotional debt.

By paying back that emotional debt, you remove your fear of being vulnerable. You move to a place of *certainity* within your own emotional space and gain the ability to communicate love to a woman.

Exercise: Pay Your Emotional Debt

This is a difficult exercise as you're going into potentially confrontational situations and looking to confront people you feel have wronged you, or those you feel you may have wronged. But this is a chance to show your vulnerability by communicating to them, "I'm willing to try harder."

1. Write down all your negative emotional debt, the instances where you have been wronged by another.
2. Reframe that negative experience into a positive. What was the positve outcome of that negative energy? (This is tough but very worth it.)
3. Now, write down any emotional debt you may have with close friends or loved ones (perhaps some people you may have wronged yourself).
4. Ask yourself: What can I do to make things up or show gratitude towards that person?
5. Make the connection with that person and allow yourself to be vulnerable.

Keep in mind that when you come clean like this and put your cards on the table, the other person may respond poorly (this can be especially true for family), but you are doing this to get closure, and no matter the result you should feel proud that you took the risk and made the effort.

How to Practise Communicating Love When You're Single

Giving a shit about people doesn't have to solely be about someone you're dating romantically. It can be about anyone you have a deeper connection with: your parents, your siblings, your close friends.

Even if it's your friends, you can still go the extra mile. If it's their birthday, it is pretty normal to get them a card and put some money in it, but where is the thought in that? No one gives a shit. But if your gift is something more personal that reminds them of something you did together, then that's 10 times more powerful and will create an emotional anchor to the object. It's not the *thing* that's important, it's the emotional memory that they can attach to it. And this is good practice for when that ideal relationship comes along.

I remember interviewing some girls in the street about how they wanted to be treated. I'll always remember this one girl. She said, "I'd rather have just one rose than a bouquet of a hundred roses."

It's a cliché, but *it's the thought that counts.*

Takeaways

You're not going to find that person you can trust with your emotions if you can't trust your own emotions and feelings. The exercises and techniques in this chapter have been developed so that *you* can come out of your shell by looking inward and figuring out why you do the things you do.

- **Look at why you're protecting yourself:** Once you understand your fears and weaknesses, you can start doing something about them.
- **Learn to show your vulnerability:** Women want someone they can connect with on an emotional level. Ultimately, we are all striving to find that person who *gets us*. Being impenetrable will only get you so far, but being honest about yourself and your flaws will enable you to make genuine connections.
- **Listen to yourself:** Find out who you are and what you believe in. You already know how awesome you are. You just need to let go of all the bullshit.
- **Give value to those who care about you:** One of the biggest steps you can take toward becoming a great man is understanding you've been put on this earth to help others. The best way to start doing that is to show those around you how you cherish them.
- **Start giving a shit:** Stop making your life about *you*. It's only those who hate themselves who consistently take from others, but being a man is about helping others feel amazing as well.

Chapter Eight: Case Study

Name: Stephen
Age: 32
Profession: Finance

What areas of your dating world did Johnny work with you on?

Johnny helped me stay in my relationship. My girlfriend and I were having a problem communicating with each other and Johnny helped me work through the mental blocks that I had in place.

How did working with Johnny on Communicating Love change your life?

Johnny showed me how to engage with my partner on an emotional level. I used to think that "being vulnerable" meant crying, but he taught me that it was about showing the other person the positive aspects of why I enjoyed being with them.

Which of the techniques that Johnny taught you do you still use on a regular basis?

I still use the journal on a day-to-day basis. Keeping a track of "relationship wins" has helped me communicate to my partner the reasons why we're together and how much I enjoy being with her.

How did working with Johnny help you outside of the dating world?

Working with others in my team. Most of the people that I work with were either scared of me or didn't want to talk to me. It's incredible to

see the change in how others interact with you once you can effectively tell them why they're useful to you and why you enjoy working with them.

What was the most valuable lesson Johnny taught you?
To be more open with my emotions.

For access to more exclusive techniques and the **'5 Seduction Secrets High-Class Women Wish You Knew'**, *www.JohnnyCassell.com/BookResources*

The Investor Mindset

"Value your time over anything else" – Johnny Cassell

The principles in this chapter will change your life. By understanding the investor way of thinking, you're going to find someone in line with your values, someone who respects your time and knows what they're looking for, so you can ultimately find the love *you're* looking for (and as a bonus become hugely attractive).

The first thing we will address is how you're using your time. Honestly, ask yourself what places you currently frequent expecting to meet the girl of your dreams. How often do you actually meet suitable candidates?

If you've been going to the same places for five years, and the girl of your dreams still hasn't walked through that door, what makes you think she's going to walk through the door next week?

You need to change your environment, so you can get a good return on your time. You have to position yourself according to where you can find high calibre women.

After reading this chapter, you'll be able to identify new, exciting environments where you can meet women more in line with your values. You will be able to look at *all* the areas of your life and see how to use your time in a way that gets you better results with women.

You will also be able to differentiate between someone who is a long-term investment and a girl who's just a bit of fun.

Story: It's About Time

You've probably noticed from my previous stories that my investor's mindset kicked in pretty early. Instead of hanging out in one area of the playground, I decided to change my environment and get a better return on my time. This practice continued into adulthood.

As I was developing my social circle back in Reading, I was let in on a little secret that Joe Public could apply for a membership at the university gym. This was great because it gave me access to a previously exclusive environment. Now I was positioned near young free-spirited university girls. (The bouncers of most of the nightclubs in Reading were in on this secret too.)

Hanging out at the gym gave me an opportunity to start being recognised around campus, giving me leverage if I wanted to attend any university parties. (You had to have an NUS card, so I always manoeuvred to be somebody's plus one.) Needless to say, I met *a lot* of girls. Sometimes I would wake up in the morning on one side of campus and be able to point out where I had woken up the weekend before.

The gym was great for networking and social leveraging, but there came a time where I exhausted these resources, and it was no longer stimulating me in the way I needed to be stimulated. I started to think, "Okay, the gym is obviously a great environment to meet women. How can I use that to position me amongst the next level of women?"

So I spent some time going around to other gyms. There were many types: weight-lifting gyms, boxersize gyms, but the one I went for in the end had everything to do with location. It was close to a business park – well-positioned for me to meet more ambitious, career-orientated women.

Sure it was four times the price of my previous gym, but it was worth it. The way I justified it was it was actually costing me more at the cheaper gym becuase I wasn't getting a good return on my time. The first day I joined, I looked through a window at a pole dancing session going on, and all I saw was a room full of gorgeous women. I spotted one other guy in the gym who knew he was also onto something good. I looked at my new buddy and said, "Shall we?" and we signed up for two classes to check out the pole dancing.

The women in that class were open-minded. Some were actually strippers, and we got to meet them without the bravado you would normally associate with walking into a strip club.

I also took evening courses. I had one evening free a week, and I asked myself, "What can I do with that free evening? I might as well learn a new skill." So I took holistic massage for two years. I was one of three guys in a class of 36 women, and I genuinely thought it was going to be a breeze. I thought I would just turn up, rub a few backs and finely toned legs, and that would be my kicks for the evening. In reality, it was an

extensive course and I had to learn a lot about anatomy. (I'm now a qualified holistic masseuse!)

Again, it's all added knowledge. It's all added value. And doing so, I positioned myself around yet another female orietated environment, and met a bank of new people I would normally never have met.

Understanding the Investor Mindset

You've probably noticed I use a lot of investor lingo in my discussion of dating and relationships. That comes from reading a lot of books on long-term financial investment, but honestly, the principles in those books translate perfectly into the dating arena. I came across a viral post that communicates the relationship between those two realms.

Supposedly, there was this young gold-digger girl from Manhattan, who had written in to this forum for wealthy businessmen and investors. She wrote an open letter that said:

I'm going to be honest of what I'm going to say here. I'm 25 this year. I'm very pretty, have style and good taste. I wish to marry a guy with $500k annual salary or above. You might say that I'm greedy, but an annual salary of $1M is considered only as middle class in New York.

My requirement is not high. Is there anyone in this forum who has an income of $500k annual salary? Are you all married? I wanted to ask: what should I do to marry rich persons like you?

Among those I've dated, the richest is $250k annual income, and it seems that this is my upper limit.

If someone is going to move into high cost residential area on the west of New York City Garden(?), $250k annual income is not enough.

I'm here humbly to ask a few questions:

1) Where do most rich bachelors hang out? (Please list down the names and addresses of bars, restaurant, gym)
2) Which age group should I target?
3) Why most wives of the riches are only average-looking? I've met a few girls who don't have looks and are not interesting, but they are able to marry rich guys.
4) How do you decide who can be your wife, and who can only be your girlfriend? (my target now is to get married)

Ms. Pretty

Supposedly the owner of J.P. Morgan replied to her message. His reply went something like this:

Dear Ms. Pretty,

I have read your post with great interest. Guess there are lots of girls out there who have similar questions like yours. Please allow me to analyse your situation as a professional investor.

My annual income is more than $500k, which meets your requirement, so I hope everyone believes that I'm not wasting time here.

From the standpoint of a business person, it is a bad decision to marry you. The answer is very simple, so let me explain.

Put the details aside, what you're trying to do is an exchange of "beauty" and "money": Person A provides beauty, and Person B pays for it, fair and square.

However, there's a deadly problem here, your beauty will fade, but my money will not be gone without any good reason. The fact is, my income might increase from year to year, but you can't be prettier year after year.

Hence from the viewpoint of economics, I am an appreciation asset, and you are a depreciation asset. It's not just normal depreciation, but exponential depreciation. If that is your only asset, your value will be much worse 10 years later.

By the terms we use in Wall Street, every trading has a position, dating with you is also a "trading position".

If the trade value dropped we will sell it and it is not a good idea to keep it for long term – same goes with the marriage that you wanted. It might be cruel to say this, but in order to make a wiser decision any assets with great depreciation value will be sold or "leased".

Anyone with over $500k annual income is not a fool; we would only date you, but will not marry you. I would advise that you forget looking for any clues to marry a rich guy. And by the way, you could make yourself to become a rich person with $500k annual income. This has better chance than finding a rich fool.

Hope this reply helps.

signed,

J.P. Morgan CEO

Whether this is a real or a satirical post, it makes a strong point: looks fade over time. There's a reason why the beauty industry is a billion-pound industry: Women are constantly struggling to maintain their youth. There's a reason why a woman's modelling career normally ends around in her mid-20s because that's when she's reached her physical peak.

We don't have to go very far to find someone with the gift of beauty. What is scarce is someone who has the qualities we're looking for.

---

*"Can't find the time? You can **always find the time** for the things that are most important to you. **Prioritise**"*
– Johnny Cassell

How to Understand True Value

In the next chapter we will talk more about knowing what you want, but for now, understand this: When you combine the investor mindset with knowing what you want, you realise the truth that beauty is common and quality is scarce. You've got to look past the looks and see what else there is in the box. Naturally, you're looking for someone who has both physical beauty and the character traits you prefer.

That's what prompted me to move to London. Reading just didn't have enough of what I was looking for. I had to be in London where I could surround myself with like-minded people – something a major city has an abundance of.

When I first heard about a recent girlfriend, I hadn't even met her yet. I just heard about certain qualities she had and

how talented she was in her field and it got me intrigued. I was so intrigued that one day, when I was at the gym with my friend, I pulled out my phone and showed him her picture and said, "This one's going to be my next girlfriend." Sure as hell, by the end of that month, she was.

The universe works in a mysterious way. If you want something, you'll be surprised how many people are willing to help you to get it. And one of those people might just be the person you were looking for.

How to Maximise Your Time

When Facebook first came out in 2004, I started seeing girls go to the hotter joints in London, Windsor, and Ascot. I showed my friends the pictures and I told them, "Let's go there" and they were like, "Why do you want to do that? We can just go to the local pub."

That didn't resonate with me. "That's not a good return on my time," I explained.

So I took it upon myself to start taking action. I moved out of that ordinary environment, acquired a wingman and started religiously going out to places where I could find better quality women.

By far the quickest way to qualify a woman is based on her physical attractiveness. By going to where more attractive women were, I increased the chances of meeting someone that fulfilled those physical traits.

That's a good start, but looks aren't enough, not if you're looking for character traits as well. So you need to screen them as you meet them. Get yourself into the headspace of keeping an eye out for the type of woman you want (using the techniques from the next chapter) and position yourself accordingly.

The Key to Good Positioning

I don't mind going to a cocktail bar where it's £10 to £15 a drink if I know the right quality women are going to be there. The price of drinks acts as a filter, so I know I'm going to get a good return on my time.

The mindset needs to change from thinking "what place in town has the best deal on drinks?" to "what place in town is the best place to meet women?". You don't mind spending more on drinks because it's the access that you're actually paying for.

Positioning is about identifying the time you have and how you can better use that time to meet the quality of women you want in your life. You need to break down every aspect of your life: the gym you go to, what classes you take, where you shop, how you commute.

Ask yourself, is your commute from home to work creating an opportunity to meet someone?

What are you doing at lunch time? Are you sitting behind your desk with your fucking packed lunch or eating at the staff canteen? Or are you out of the whole building where you can position yourself in that cute little café next to the publishing house where you see all the cute PR people and models? How you choose to position yourself directly affects the kind of women you're going to meet.

Think about positioning in terms of you being a brand. Imagine you see Hackett (premium menswear) partnering

up with Aston Martin (luxury car manufacturer). That partnership makes sense because they both have a similar type of clientele.

In the same way, once you start seeing yourself as a high-quality man, you're going to want to partner with a high-quality woman. You are both incredible individually, but when you come together you're going to be a force to be reckoned with.

Think about the bigger picture. You've got to think about who your target audience is and then think about who you need to be associated with to get access to those people. Then you've got to do your homework and find the places that will give you the results.

For example, if you like models, you should position yourself accordingly. Put yourself around club promoters, photographers, and fashion designers, so you can build that social wealth and grow that network.

By focusing on your positioning, you're going to live a better lifestyle. You're going to go to better places, eat better food, hang out with more like-minded, high-quality people, and as a result, you're going to lead a much more attractive lifestyle.

Once you start living the life *you* want, you're going to meet people (not just women) who want the same. And you'll be more likely to meet those women with the rare qualities you're looking for. You're going to attract the woman who shares those same values.

"Don't make the mistake of putting the key to your happiness in someone else's pocket" – Johnny Cassell

---

Techniques:

How to Not Waste Time

If I'm going out with a client, I won't spend more than five minutes (unless I anticipate it will pick up) in a venue I feel is not giving me a good return on my time. If I've got one evening to go out, I'm not going to spend time in a bar with no women. I'm going to move to the next venue, and the next, till I find a good place.

If you're starting out, there's going to be some trial and error, so you'll need to go out every night to explore. Everyone needs to do their homework in terms of what a particular environment yields.

Note which venues brought you what results. Which places had more of the women you're looking for? Which venues attraced women that visually stimualted you? Which bars, clubs, or activities had a large amount of women with characteristics you value?

If you're looking to smash this aspect of your life, then you have to work backwards:

- Where am I meeting the right girls?
- Where am I getting the numbers?
- What environment is providing me with the right entertainment, the right energy?
- Where am I having the best time?

The first month of you trying to crack any new environment shouldn't really be about you meeting women. It should be about doing that homework. Going there, meeting the right

people, and seeing if a particular venue is providing the right content. If it's not, then it's the wrong place. Get out of there.

Takeaways

Time is the most precious resource you have. Every single day you waste doing the wrong things, hanging out in the wrong places, and spending time with the wrong people is literally time wasted. It's not coming back.

- **Maximise your time:** Analyse your results. If a certain action or place isn't giving you the return you want, ditch it. Time is your most precious resource.
- **Beauty is common:** Sure, you want to be with someone you're sexually attracted to, but what about the long game? The investor mindset helps you understand that you're in this for the long-haul. Qualify women based on their personality.
- **Value action:** One of the reasons my girlfriend was so attractive was because of the things she had done. Most people are all talk. Look at their actions to determine if they are worth your time.
- **Positioning is everything:** Where are you going to meet the woman you want? Go to places you think they'll hang out. If they aren't there, go somewhere else.
- **Focus on** you: Although I learned holistic massage (and pole dancing) to meet women, I focussed on improving *me*. One of the most attractive qualities in a man is continual self-improvement.

Chapter Nine: Case Study

Name: Michael
Age: 34
Profession: Real Estate Developer

What areas of your dating world did Johnny work with you on?

Johnny worked with me mainly with approach anxiety and Inner Game. Most importantly, I learned how to market myself better and convey value.

How did working with Johnny on developing an Investor Mindset change your life?

Johnny encouraged me to focus on my "target market" where I believed the girls I like the most can be found. I mainly focused on Chelsea, London and Stockholm, Sweden. The initial investments (accommodation, flights etc.) paid off very soon and I cannot stress enough how satisfied I am to have taken both the financial and time investments, since they fast-tracked the whole process and strongly increased the chance of meeting the girl I want to be with in the long run.

Which of the techniques that Johnny taught you do you still use on a regular basis?

When talking to girls, I definitely use a lot of Johnny-style cheekiness and dirty-talk in a sophisticated/gentleman way! I would summarise it as going under the radar at first, wolf-in-sheep-skin attitude.

How did working with Johnny help you outside of the dating world?

I believe I generally gained more confidence and acquired a go-getter attitude, in all kinds of social environments. Humour plays a crucial role.

What was the most valuable lesson Johnny taught you?
Most importantly, I learned from Johnny how not to be intimidated by any kind of social setting or crowd or any girl who is a straight 10. I learned not to back-off but tackle these situations with confidence and, over time, learn to even enjoy them.

To learn more about constructing your Elite Seduction lifestyle, head over to *www.JohnnyCassell.com/BookResources*, where you'll find exclusive techniques and access to the **'5 Seduction Secrets High-Class Women Wish You Knew'**.

How to Discover What You Really Want

"Love yourself first and everything else falls into line"
- Johnny Cassell

Dating is a serious journey like any other. You have to go out and experience women before you can firm up the picture of what it is you're looking for. I always say, "You need to taste all the flavours on the menu until you know what you like eating."

In my early days of seduction, I was meeting a lot of women. I was breaking down and understanding all the stages of sleeping with women because I wanted to figure out the process. Then, whenever I met an attractive woman, I was ready because I could work through that process automatically.

Remember the girl I met in the shopping mall all those years ago? She was basically "plastic fantastic". I found that attractive because I had a lack of reference. I now have a much more refined taste, which I wouldn't have if I hadn't endulged in all those experiences.

In this chapter, you're going to reflect on what it is *you* want, but first you need to understand and recognise what you *don't* want.

Story: The Secret Origins of Johnny Cassell

I remember the first time I realized my friends' outlook wasn't the same as mine. I was still at school, and after school, my friends and I were…well…a bunch of jackasses. We'd throw ourselves in bushes whilst filming ourselves and piss around on skateboards. I couldn't even skate, so you can imagine how horrendous that looked.

I enjoyed doing all those things. It was boy stuff. But when these guys started getting interested in girls, the girls they went after were the exact kind of girls you would imagine a bunch of jackasses would be interested in.

I recall a time where we all went to "hang out" with some of these girls. We were walking towards the meeting spot, and I just knew there was nothing I wanted from these people. At their core, these women were small-minded, and their greatest aspiration was to get knocked-up as quickly as possible. I didn't fancy becoming a father at the tender age of 15, nor did I want to be with a foul-mouthed girl from the hood.

So I stopped myself in my tracks and I said ,"I'm going to get back for dinner." That was the moment I decided to sever my ties with those people and sought to replace them with people more in tune with who I was. I found a different group of friends and began spending more time with guys more in line with my values.

We are all different and looking for different things. We all have different wants and different needs, but if you're going to live a life in line with your values, you first need to know what they are.

Technique:

Exercise: Build Your Ideal Woman

This is not an easy exercise, but it's an exercise I do with every single person I work with. And this is an exercise you must do *right now* if you want more clarity about what you're attracted to.

We did this exercise at the beginning of the book, but it's time to do it again in more detail using everything you've learned. After reading this book, your mindset has shifted, and now you've got the skillset to make your wildest dreams come true.

Understand, you can have *anything* you want in life. You just have to put yourself in the right place and position yourself around the right people. I guarantee the first time we did this exercise you held back because you were scared of sharing what you truly want, but if there's one thing you should take away

from this book it's that until you accept what you want and state it clearly, you're going to be staying mired in mediocrity.

Take a sheet of A4 paper and divide it down the middle.

The first list we're going to make is a visual list. On one half of the paper, write "Visual" at the top. Now write down all the visual qualities you're attracted to. The key thing here is detail.

I'm talking everything.

How tall is she is compared to you? What about her skin tone? What kind of complexion does she have? Is she tanned? Is she Mediterranean? Is she porcelain white?

What's her hair like? Is it blonde, brunette? Is she a redhead? What race is she? Is she white? Mixed? Asian? Black? What are her features?

When you look at her face, what are you instantly drawn towards? What shape face does she have? Is it more elongated? Does she have more of an oval face? Does she have soft or prominent cheek bones? What about her lips? Are they smaller or quite full? How does she wear her makeup?

Is your attention instantly drawn to her eyes? If so, have a look. What draws you in? Is it her eye colour? That smoky look of hers? Is it the colour of eyeshadow she uses?

How does she wear her hair? What body shape does she have? Is she quite slim? Toned? Voluptuous? Is she an A cup, a B cup, a C cup, a D cup?

What about her posture? (I'm a sucker for posture. It's a big thing for me.) How does she hold herself? Is she toned? If so, what parts of her body are toned? How does she dress?

It's likely you haven't thought about a lot of these things before. If we were to ask your friends, "What's your type?" they'd probably say "hot". That's so vague. That person is going to settle for an average woman because "hot" women are everywhere.

One guy who did really well at describing this list was an artist. Everything he said was so poetic. It was amazing, I was desperate to fucking meet his imagined woman. She was that great.

Okay, that's just one side of the list.

On the other half of your sheet write "Character". Now lets think about her character traits and how they match your values.

Think about what's important to you. Is it religion? Do you belong to a faith? Is it important that she's part of that same practice?

Is she driven? Challenging? Opinionated? Does she have her own social circle? What social tribe would you say she belongs to? Is she the leader or more of a follower? Does she have her own hobbies and interests? What are they? Is she well-cultured? Well-travelled?

Is she motivated in her career? If so, what does she do? Is she more of an entrepreneurial person or more of a professional?

How is she sexually? What is her experience in terms of sexuality? What does she like? How open-minded is she? Does she want kids? How many?

Is she creative? What's her political stance? Does she enjoy clubbing or pubbing? What about her taste in music? Is it similar to yours? Does she *need* to have *any* taste in music?

I want to reiterate: detail is the key, and those details need to be authentic to *what you want.*

By now you should have two pretty detailed lists, but go ahead and expand those lists on your own. But keep in mind, the following words are banned from your lists: "good", "beautiful" and "nice". Those are generic words, and they are absolutely meaningless.

With both your lists, don't let your mind get in the way of what you want. If you want to date a high-powered, dominant in the boardroom but submissive in the bedroom, blonde, with DD breasts, and a PhD, then write all those traits down. If you see a particular quality in a woman and find yourself thinking, "I could date someone like that," then you *need* to write down that trait. I'll explain why in a second.

Your lists will help you understand what it is you're looking for in great detail. They can also show you how you compliment a woman. If you look at your visual list, those are all fantastic compliments, unique to your criteria.

When you do realise you've met someone you like, and she has one of the traits you've written on your list, your compliment is going to pack more of a punch. She's heard "You're really beautiful," a million times, but she has probably never heard, "Your purfume really matches your personality". A specific compliment like that is more genuine because you've thought about it and genuinely mean it.

These lists are powerful. With them, you have created qualification material you are now aware of when you go out meeting people. Now, you can have a compelling conversation about hobbies you're both interested in. You can have a stimulating conversation about passions you share. You can escalate by using the visual side of the list by commenting on something she has that you like. Most importanly, you can see if she has the character traits you're looking for. We'll talk about how to do that in a second.

Look at the lists again. What for you is the bigger list? Is it the visual list or the character trait list? If it's quite evident that the visual list is bigger than the qualities list, then it's evident you're putting women on a pedestal based on their looks. You need to shift that perspective.

You need to see a woman's looks as her wrapping paper only. You don't know anything about her yet. You're going over there to speak to her to see if there's anything more beneath the surface.

Until you know more about a woman's character, the highest rating you can give her is a five (this is a little game I play). But if it seems like there is more substance to her, and she does have more qualities from the character list, then you know what? She might actually be an eight. She might be a nine. I personally don't think tens exist. But you know what? She might even be a 10.

One thing you need to remember, and this is most important, is that you are a 12. If you don't believe you're a 12, then you're always going to feel inferior to any high quality woman you pursue. She needs for you to understand that you *are* a 12; otherwise, she's going to go and find someone who is. That's because she needs someone who's going to take the lead in a relationship.

"Every partner is a warm up until you find the right one"
– Johnny Cassell

How to Become a 12

You have to be realistic with yourself. You can have a successful relationship with that buxom CEO with the PhD, but you have to *be* the man she's looking for. If you're an overweight guy

earning £10,000, who lives with your elderly mother, there's a much lower chance she's going to go for you.

Money isn't everything, but *enough* money is important because it conveys one of the most attractive qualities a man can have: security. If you're living below the average person's means, you're out of the game already because you're not promising to add value. You're potentially taking value because you're asking for her to step down from a lifestyle she's used to living. She's not a gold-digger. You're a lazy fuck.

With that said, if your monetary value is there yet you need to provide value elsewhere. That may be having interesting hobbies, intelligence, humour, or a sense of adventure. If you're in a situation that doesn't reflect your inner world of what you want, you need to start asking yourself some questions.

If this applies to you, ask yourself why you are in that situation. Why are you overweight? Why are you still living at home? Why don't you have a job that not only provides a means and a way of living for yourself, but has the capacity to look after your nearest and dearest.

Before you get that 10, this book should be a motivator for you to become a 12. You need to look at your lifestyle. You need to look at the areas of your life you feel you can improve on.

Make a list of all the things that make you great. Now make a list of what you need to change, and what you're going to change, after reading this book. Take some time to **answer these questions** and check in on them every three to six months:

- What are you great at?
- What can you change?
- What restaurants do you eat at?
- What places do you frequently visit?

- How much do you weigh?
- Have you gained/lost weight?
- Have you put on muscle?
- Have you become more fit?
- Have you become more eloquent in speech?
- Are you learning a new language?
- Have you travelled?
- How have you positioned yourself in terms of where you live and what you want?

If you find out you're fed up with living in a small town, move to where you can be around more abundance. If you want to become more confident, start learning a combat sport. If you want to increase your wealth, make smarter investments with your money. If you want to be more like James Bond, enroll in a stunt driving course.

These are just examples. You need to be creative and *choose* who you want to be.

The questions you need to be asking yourself are "What can I do to 10x my life?" "What can I do to move closer to becoming a 12?".

If you took the time to make those lists, take another moment and think about how you're going to spend your next six months. Now that you have a list of things you're going to do, figure out how you're going to do them.

Take action. Open a calendar on your phone or on your wall and start writing when you're going to start doing the things on your list.

- When will you scout those local gyms?
- When are you going to find, and sign up for that French class?
- When are you going to book that weekend in Barcelona?

- When will you interview those three personal trainers and choose your favourite?
- When are you going to read that book about psychology that's been on your shelf for years?

It's all about deciding to do something and then doing it. Chisel yourself into the kind of man who deserves your ideal woman. If you're not willing to be the best you for her, then why should she bother to be the best her for you?

Why You Do the Things You Do

It's a known fact that man's main driver is sex. We are all looking to reproduce, and we're looking for that suitable partner. A woman wants the most valuable sperm. She is here to reproduce, but she's looking for the strongest sperm in the bank, so to speak.

If you want examples of this in public, look at the way men use women to propel them towards success.

Rumour has it Richard Branson bought Necker Island on the back of trying to impress the girl he was dating at the time. They jumped in a helicopter, and called out his real estate agent to go and look at some islands to buy. Branson wasn't really interested in the island, so he put in a ridiculously low offer

Twelve months later, Branson got a call back to say if he slightly increased the offer to $120,000 he could have the island. You know that story, right? It's true.

No matter what experiences you have with women, good or bad, you always have to reframe those experiences in a positive light because it's always going to push you to do better.

Accordingly, if women are looking for the best sperm, you should be looking for the best womb – the woman you think would be a good mother to your child – someone not just fertile and attractive, but someone aligned with your values.

"No girl that loves you wants you to give up on your dreams. Never give up on your dreams."
– Johnny Cassell

Goals Aren't Just on the Pitch

There's a saying that will always haunt me: "If you fail to plan, you plan to fail."

That adage haunts me because when I was studying motorsport engineering, I had an end of year project to build a go-kart from scratch and only a vague plan of what I was doing. I sourced this vintage go-kart frame and various bits and pieces, and my schoolmates and I just went to work. There never was a time when we sat down and planned. We just ran with what we had. As a consequence, we never made the deadline. The project overran and took far longer than expected.

Since then, I've always taken having goals a lot more seriously. It's one of those things when you grow up that you never pay attention to. Even in my primary school, I remember hearing about goal setting, but thinking it was just a fucking waste of time. Later on though, I realised how important this

goal-setting stuff really was, especially when I started my journey in self-development.

If you're not quantifying your goals, then you've got nothing to keep you accountable. If you find you keep going back to square one, it's because you're not writing down your objectives. If you're on the same financial level for years upon years and you've still got the same amount in the bank it's because you've not giving yourself direction and setting firm benchmarks.

You've not giving yourself that kick up the backside. The only reason I feel I've experienced success in this life is because I was incredibly driven toward change. After I started recording all my dating successes, no matter how big or small (using the Pocket Diary from Chapter Two), I took that same method into other areas of my life I was looking to fulfill. I now take the same principle to my business life.

When I set myself goals but don't record what I've been doing, those goals go to shit. Part of that is not being aware of the progress I *am* making.

For example, I set myself a goal once to invest in property. My friend knew about this., so come the year's end, he asked how the project was going. I had to admit, I didn't know.

So he had me lay it all out for him, and I told him everything: how I sorted out my books, found a mortgage broker and how the mortgage criteria changed. "It's just been one long, long journey," I said, somewhat despondent.

"Right," he responded. Then he pointed to a vase on the table that was full of stones, pebbles, and sand and said, "If you take the contents out of this vase and put it in back in again, how would you do it?"

"Well," I said, "I would put the pebbles in first. Then I'd put in the stones, and then the sand."

I knew where he was going with the metaphor. He was saying I'd done the bigger things. I'd put all the building blocks in place but I was just a few speckles of sand away from actually punching through to the next stage and completing the project. And he was right.

So why didn't I feel it?

The answer was simple. Up until then, I hadn't been recording my successes in that area of my life. I wasn't writing down the steps I'd taken to move myself forward in real estate. That left me in despair, feeling empty and unfulfilled because I had just focused on what I *didn't have* rather than what I *had* already done.

This is true in the seduction arena as well. You're going to have nights where you don't perform well. But if you've been recording your efforts, if you have that bank of positive reference points, then the confidence you feel is going to push you through to the next stage.

So set goals for yourself, and reward yourself for doing so, because lack of goalsetting is just going to give you anxiety, and further down the road, that can lead to depression.

In the beginning of your journey, your goals may simply be to "talk to five new women a night", but as you progress, you can set new goals like, "get five kiss-closes in a night". Ultimately, *you* control how fast you go on this journey. By doing the exercises and practising the techniques, your journey through the world of seduction and dating is going to accelerate until you've built up your skillset and are ready to meet the woman of your dreams.

Takeaways

For some, knowing what they want is a case of trial and error. For others, they know exactly want they want early on in life. Your mission is to discover exactly what it is you've been born to do.

You may have noticed that the final chapters of this book haven't been as focussed on women. That's because, before you can find your ideal woman, you're going to have to create the life *you* want *first*.

- **Become the man** you **want to be:** If you want to travel, *do* it. If you want to become wealthy, that's on *you*. Create the life you've dreamed of and the women will follow.
- **Write down what you want:** Until you know what you want, you're going to be wasting your time. So be specific about your desires. We did that exercise with women, but you can use it with every aspect of your life.
- **Set goals:** Without targets, you're not going to feel the satisfaction of completing what you've set out to do. Set goals so you have targets to hit, and record and celebrate those victories.

Chapter Ten: Case Study

Name: Gunter
Age: 44
Profession: Investment Banker/Programmer

What areas of your dating world did Johnny work with you on?

Approaching women in the day, his influence is more from the perspective of understanding values and making sure that there's a deeper connection with a woman than just hitting on them.

How did working with Johnny on understanding what exactly you want from your existence change your life?

I was able to be more direct and more focused in my interactions with women. He gave my ship a rudder and through knowing the direction that I wanted to go in I was able to get more success.

When I say "success" I mean get the number and develop a connection more long term. I really struggled with it before.

Which of the techniques that Johnny taught you do you still use on a regular basis?

Identify with values. We did a session on learning how to identify values within myself and my partners.

The partner that I've just come out of a relationship with, as time went by it was easy to see (thanks to Johnny) that our values were diverging, and it gave me a point at which I could move on.

How did working with Johnny help you outside of the dating world?

Communicating. Just learning how to talk to people in an easier and more relaxed manner. I was very rigid with conversation, asking the standard questions, "What's your name?", "Where are you from?" and so on.

Now I can come from a place of fluidity and not come across like I'm interviewing the other person.

I can actually now actively participate in conversations and not make it seem like I'm interrogating the other person.

What was the most valuable lesson Johnny taught you?

Confidence. I admire his constant evolution in himself and I've learned how to be real with myself.

For more resources and access to **'5 Seduction Secrets High-Class Women WISH you knew'**, head over to *www.JohnnyCassell.com/BookResources*

Conclusion

Congratulations on making it this far! Now comes the real challenge. You've got to go out there and implement these techniques and record your successes, no matter how big or small they are. Give yourself that pat on the back for taking action.

What's great about you now is that you're amongst the small percentage of people who have *chosen* to take action in this area of their life. You've chosen to make a positive change. You've chosen to have more high-calibre women in your life. You've decided to build up your social value and move yourself away from the small town minds plaguing you with *their* insecurities. You've chosen to position yourself around people who understand that reality is what we make it.

But what does it say about you if you don't go out there and apply what you have learned? You are now in the SAS of seduction. You have a skillset that 99 per cent of the other men out there haven't bothered to learn.

If you start implementing what you've read (and you already should have) your perception of the world is going to change. You'll see all the mistakes the other guys are making, and you'll

see when someone is interested in you. Ultimately, you'll see that *you* build the fairy tale of your life.

There's a whole bunch of women out there who are *frustrated*. They *do* settle for certain men out of convenience. They *do* settle for shitty guys who don't want to learn how to communicate better. They *do* settle for men who don't respect themselves enough to improve areas in which they're weak.

There's this beautiful gift out there: Seduction. If you have the ability to give someone that experience of meeting an incredible man and building a real life love story and you're *not* doing it, it's you that's being selfish. Don't throw that gift away.

I've shared a lot of stories with you in this book, and the reason why I did that is so you can understand that *you* can lead a similar life. Besides, I get my kicks telling stories about my students.

On that note, I'm so excited to hear all of the adventures you're going to be getting into in the coming months and years after reading this book. So send me an email (**info@johnnycassell.com**) or visit my website **www.johnnycassell.com**.

Here's one final gift to you guys who have completed this book: a 30-minute consultation with one of my team *on the house*. Mention the codeword "Patronova" in your email and we'll sort that out for you.

Thanks again for coming on this journey.

Johnny Cassell

The Programs

Impactful Connection Workshop

For: Those that want to dip their toe in the water and get a feel for the coaching

Outcome: Understand the basics of being an Elite Seducer (including how to approach women in the day/night, how to have an enthralling conversation, mastering your online game, and much more)

- Have a team of Wingmen supporting your approaches at top London hot spots
- A crash course in everything Women WISHED you knew
- Learn the Elite Seduction system in the day, implement the system in the night

Immersive Transformation Experience

For: Those who want to break away from old habits and establish a solid foundation moving forward

Outcome: More phone numbers than you'll know what to do with! Seven days and seven nights of working with one of the UK's Top Dating Coaches on a bespoke course tailored toward creating the lifestyle of an Elite Seducer

- Have Johnny supporting your approaches at top London night clubs seven nights in a row!
- A deep dive into everything Women WISHED you knew
- Learn the Elite Seduction system in the day, implement the system in the night
- In-depth analysis of your individual psychological sticking points
- Bespoke program created specifically to solve your sticking points

Elite Seducer Mentorship

For: Those ready to join the exclusive circle of Elite Seducers and build an awe inspiring life for themselves (and as many lucky ladies as you choose)

Outcome: Complete lifestyle transformation. Work directly with Johnny for six to twelve months building a lifestyle that magnetically attracts your dream woman. This is not just about building confidence with women, this is a full blown holistic self-development programme based in progressive momentum.

- Have Johnny supporting your approaches at top London night clubs both in person and via your phone
- A crash course in everything Women WISHED you knew

- Learn the Elite Seduction system in the day, implement the system in the night
- In-depth analysis of your individual psychological sticking points
- Bespoke program created specifically to solve your sticking points
- Elite Seduction habit creation making it literally IMPOSSIBLE to NOT attract High-Class women into your life
- Access to Johnny's network of High-Class individuals (including: the owner of the UK's most notorious sex parties, numerous multi-millionaires, and men that have gone through your exact journey)

For more details about how you can work with Johnny, head over to *www.johnnycassell.com*

Acknowledgments

We are where we are as a result of those who have been in our lives past and present. The brain is like a sponge and it absorbs influence, ideas and direction on a day to day basis. Whether of a negative reference or of a positive one, it is important to express gratitude to those who we are conscious of that fall into these categories.

Mother

Thank you for being supportive of my vision, raising me and being the kindest, loveliest mother I could ever wish for. Your upbringing, your pain and what you went through growing up all plays a part in who I am today. I love you with all my heart and never a day goes by that I don't appreciate your presence in my life.

I think it's also important to mention how thankful I am of you putting up with my bedroom parties every weekend when I used to live at home. People just used to keep on turning up and all you wanted to do was sit there in peace and quiet, watching Strictly Come Dancing! Stories I still share in my workshops today.

My father

One of the hardest things that I have had to do in my life was walk away from the family business to go and work on my own business. I thank you for exposing me to the world of entrepreneurism, hard work and graft. You have been key to my success and I am eternally grateful for all you have given. You are one hell of father.

Adam

My dear brother, I am forever grateful to you for putting your energy towards various writing projects including this one.

My Wingmen

Louis, James, Lloyd and for many who would chose to keep their days with me a secret in case their girlfriends and wives have a certain opinion of it all… I get it. You know who you all are. Thank you for putting up with my obsession and drive. Without you guys at the beginning, I wouldn't have had anyone to bounce off of.

My Clients

Thank you for choosing me as your coach and mentor. Without your trust and overcoming of certain scepticism that outlies that, we would not have been able to embark on the journeys that we have gone on together. There are so many stories. I truly love what I do and am thankful for being able to meet each and every one of you.

A very special thank you to my clients who gave their time to share their story for each case study featured in this book.

My team

You guys are doing an incredible job at serving our clients and doing the world a good. Every year we grow and more challenges come our way and we give our clients an amazing experience. Well done! Special thanks to Dave who has been by my side right from the early days.

Spinex

Andrew Garbett and the lovely team down at Spinex for fixing my back and keeping me in work. You guys are magicians!

Emma Sayle

You and your team are doing a remarkable and inspiring job over at Killing Kittens and it's always a joy to speak to all the Kittens and Toms at the workshop events. Your ambition, drive and message stands tall, shaping society into a healthier environment for females alike.

Nate Chai

I have to thank Nate for sitting down with me and getting this book formatted and out on the page for you guys to read. Quite a painstaking process and with many delays due to putting my clients first but we got there in the end. Thank you.

Friends in the nightlife scene

Too many to list here. Whenever I go out I am always made to feel like I am home. I appreciate your hospitality and the playgrounds you have provided for myself and my clients over the years.

Julia Loesch

Julia, you and your highly skilled team shot a fantastic Documentary on the Galileo network, 'This Is How The World Falls In Love'. Beautifully shot, with such care and elegance. If only you did a follow up as the client I was working with is now married!

Nils Casjens

Nils, you and your team shot a very honest piece for your documentary that featured on ARTE TV in Germany. I think you captured a great piece that allowed me to have a voice in such a confusing climate for men in the height of the #metoo campaign. Thank you, you are a man of your word.

And finally, all my colleagues I have worked with, teachers and mentors in any shape or form.

Thank you.

About the Author

Johnny Cassell helps individuals become their better selves and taps into a plethora of social tools to better their dating and social lives.

Here are just three of his personal highlights:

1. Within 6 months of joining Johnny's mentorship programme, Jay went from a geeky shut-in to a social butterfly with a life purpose and was married to the woman of his dreams within 6 months. Initially, he was super-sceptical and wouldn't turn up to sessions. Johnny ambushed him in a hotel and got him back and gave him the self-belief to change his world.

2. One of the more unusual examples of how Johnny's mentorship has changed lives was a parent. The parent told Johnny that after working with him and unlocking his emotional availabilty and learning to express those emotions in a healthy way, his relationship with his son improved.

3. The complete mental transformation of Keri. Keri was, by his own admission, obese and he was holding onto

the mental perception of that. Through working with Johnny, Keri was able to build the mental resilience and confidence to not only approach beautiful women, but ask for promotions, and live life on his terms.

Through his immersive style programmes, he ensures that all his students leave with the necessary confidence and self esteem they need to attract the women they desire into their lives. By looking at mindset, social intuition, conversational abilities that stimulate others, Johnny enables his clients to build an attractive lifestyle that is filled with joy for both yourself and your chosen partner.

Ultimately he spends a lot of time with the individuals making sure they're a good investment for their future partners and to identify a good investment when they see one.

When he works with the clients, it's a bespoke and holistic process. The clients work with highly skilled individuals who are experts in their field. It's not just the social skills, it's the complete lifestyle, the whole package from the ground up.

For what started out as a need for himself in the early days, he originally didn't want to share his newfound knowledge with anyone. It was only when he started helping his friends that he realised the joy in seeing them get over their limited beliefs.

Johnny took that passion and ran with it into what is now a global operation, running workshops and private coaching solutions to individuals all around the world.

His goal is to change as many people's lives as he possibly can during his time here on Planet Earth.